IN THE

HEART OF INDIA

OR

Beginnings of Missionary Work in Bundela Land

IN THE

HEART OF INDIA

OR

Beginnings of Missionary Work in Bundela Land

WITH A SHORT CHAPTER ON THE CHARACTERISTICS OF BUNDELKHAND AND ITS PEOPLE, AND FOUR CHAPTERS OF JHANSI HISTORY

JAMES F. HOLCOMB, D. D.

AND

HELEN H. HOLCOMB

GYAN

Published by

Gyan Publishing House
5, Ansari Road
Daryaganj, New Delhi-110002
Phone: 011-47034999, 9811692060
E-mail: books@gyanbooks.com

Distribution Network
gyanbooks.com
India, USA, Canada, UK, Australia, France

ISBN: 978-81-212-8987-0 (PB)
First Published, 1905

2nd Impression 2023

Printed at: Gyan Press, Delhi.

IN THE HEART OF INDIA *OR* Beginnings of Missionary Work in Bundela Land

AUTHORS: JAMES F. HOLCOMB AND HELEN H. HOLCOMB

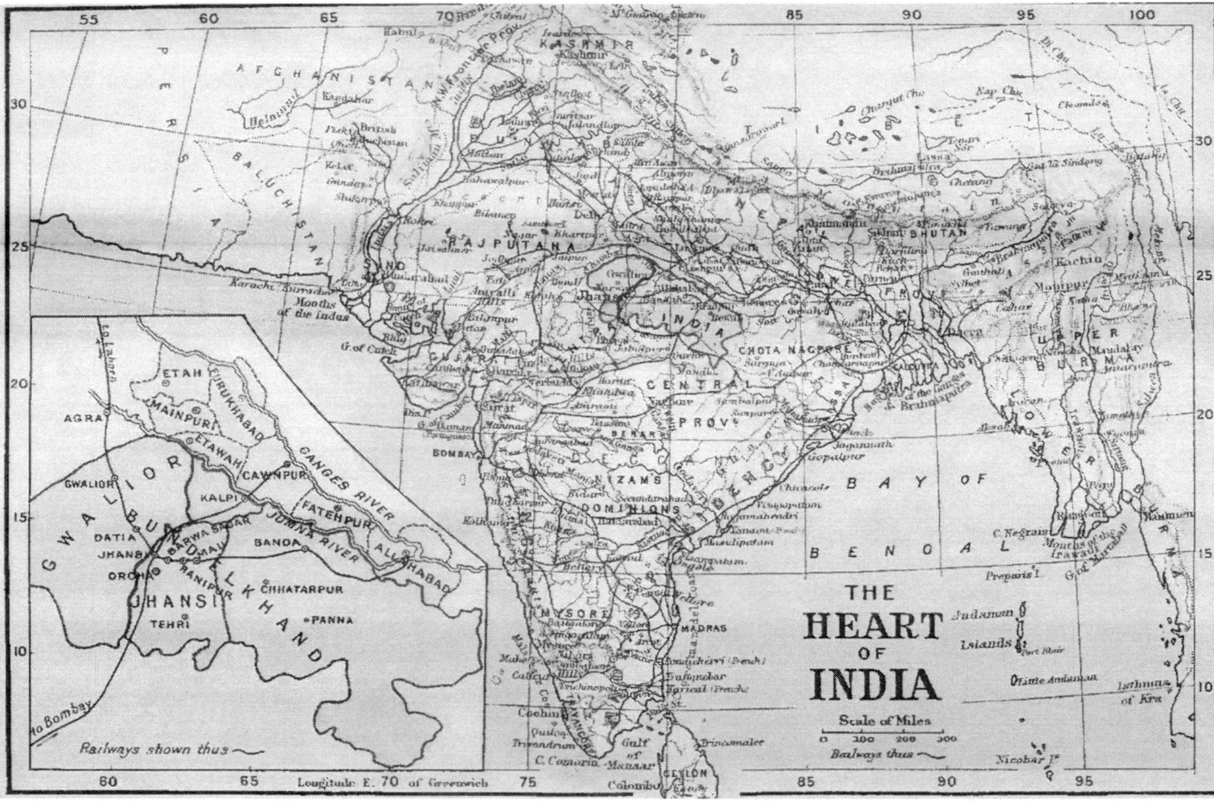
THE HEART OF INDIA
Scale of Miles
Railways thus
Railways shown thus
Longitude E. 70 of Greenwich
AFGHANISTAN
BALUCHISTAN
PERSIA
RAJPUTANA
SIND
KASHMIR
CENTRAL INDIA
CENTRAL PROVS
CHOTA NAGPORE
NIZAM'S DOMINIONS
MYSORE
BERAR
BHUTAN
UPPER BURMA
LOWER BURMA
BAY OF BENGAL
BOMBAY
MADRAS
CALCUTTA
CEYLON
Andaman Islands
G. of Cutch
Mouths of the Indus
GWALIOR
BUNDELKHAND
AGRA
ETAH
MAINPURI
FURUKHABAD
ETAWAH
CAWNPUR
KALPI
GANGES RIVER
JUMNA RIVER
FATEHPUR
ALLAHABAD
DATIA
JHANSI
ORCHA
RANIPUR
BANDA
CHHATARPUR
PANNA
TEHRI
to Bombay
to Lahore

A QUIET DELL IN JHANSI.

IN THE HEART OF INDIA

OR

Beginnings of Missionary Work in Bundela Land

WITH A SHORT CHAPTER ON THE CHARACTERISTICS OF BUNDELKHAND AND ITS PEOPLE, AND FOUR CHAPTERS OF JHANSI HISTORY

BY

JAMES F. HOLCOMB, D. D.

AND

HELEN H. HOLCOMB

PHILADELPHIA
THE WESTMINSTER PRESS
1905

TO THE

Officers and Members of the Executive Committee

OF THE

Woman's Foreign Missionary Society of the Presbyterian Church

Who, by their encouragement and generous gifts,
laid the foundation of this mission station
in the Heart of India

This Volume is Gratefully and Affectionately Dedicated

EXPLANATORY FOREWORD

A word of explanation seems to be demanded in regard to the make-up of this little book.

The reason for writing this unpretentious volume was found in the circumstance that when we were in the homeland, twelve years ago, and gave on a number of occasions an account of our beginning at Jhansi, those who listened to the narrative were unmistakably interested in it; but chiefly it was found in the opinion expressed by valued friends of our common cause, who listened to the story, that it would be well worth while to put it into print for the sake of those interested in our work who would not have an opportunity of hearing it, and not only for the sake of those already interested in our particular field, but of others whose interest might be enlisted by the perusal of it.

It was not till the larger portion of the book, beginning with Chapter IX, had been written, that it occurred to us that as this was a book giving an account of beginnings of missionary work in the heart of India, it would be well to make mention of what others before us had done in the way of pioneering in this same field; and also to give a brief description of the characteristics of Bundela Land and its people.

And finally, as the founding of the city of Jhansi as the capital of a new principality, and its subsequent history, culminating in the events of 1857 and 1858, were of unusual interest, it was decided to devote four additional chapters to these topics; not the least motive for writing these chapters being that of showing the kind of stuff of which some of the women of India are made.

EXPLANATORY FOREWORD

CONTENTS

LIST OF ILLUSTRATIONS

I.

WORK BEGUN IN THE EASTERN PORTION.

1841-42.

* Bundela Land is known in India as Bundelkhand, which means the portion of the Bundelas. The districts of Allahabad, Fatehpur, Cawnpore, Furrukhabad, Etah, Mainpuri and Etawah comprise that portion of the Furrukhabad Mission field which lies in the Doab, meaning the land of the two waters, the two waters being the two great rivers, the Ganges on the north, and the Jumna on the south. Bundelkhand has for its northern boundary the Jumna river, and from south-east to north-west is conterminous with that part of the Furrukhabad Mission field which lies in the Jumna-Ganges Doab. No other mission stands in such close proximity to Bundelkhand as the Furrukhabad Mission. The city of Allahabad is at the south-eastern end of the Doab, being at the junction of the Ganges and Jumna rivers. The city of Etawah is on the river Jumna at the distance of 206 miles north-west of Allahabad. The city of Fatehpur is situated between the two rivers, being 70 miles north-west of Allahabad.

What could be more natural than that the American Presbyterian missionaries at the stations of Allahabad, Fatehpur and Etawah should look out towards the

---

* Pronounced Boondeyla.

unevangelized millions of Bundelkhand with a special and prayerful interest?

The city of Jhansi, which is in the geographical centre of India, is also centrally situated in Bundelkhand. The other chief cities of this territory are Gwalior* in the west, and Banda in the east. Banda is only 40 miles from Fatehpur, and only 30 miles from the Jumna river, which forms the southern boundary of the Fatehpur district.

Allahabad was the second place in India which the Presbyterian Church of the U. S. A. was led to choose as a mission station; Ludhiana in the Punjab, or land of the five waters, having been the first station in India to be established by the pioneer representatives of that Church. The first missionaries at Ludhiana longed to cross the Sutledge and carry the Gospel to the Sikhs; and equally eager were the first missionaries at Allahabad to spread the knowledge of Christ among the people on the other side of the Jumna. Accordingly we find them forming and putting into execution such plans as were then feasible for giving the Gospel to the inhabitants of Bundelkhand.

The earliest of the American Presbyterian missionaries stationed at Allahabad were the Rev. James McEwen (1836), the Rev. James Wilson and the Rev. J. H. Morrison (1838), the Rev. Joseph Warren (1839), and the Rev. Joseph Owen (1841). As early as the cold season 1841-42 the Rev. James Wilson, accompanied by the Rev. Joseph Owen, made a two months' preaching tour in the Doab and Bundelkhand. The chief part of these two months was spent in Bundelkhand, and of this portion

* Gwalior, though not now considered a part of Bundelkhand, was once included in Bundela Land, the territory of the Bundela Chief, Chhatarsal, having extended as far toward the north-west at the Chumbal river.

of their tour Mr. Wilson gave the following account:—"We visited Kalpi, Hamirpur, Banda, and other large places, besides a great multitude of smaller villages on the way. At each of the larger places we stopped several days, in the smaller places generally only one day. At Kalpi and at Banda we had interesting discussions with a Pandit or learned Hindu, and a Maulavi or learned Musalman. These were such as to give us pleasing evidences that Christianity is making steady and distinct advances in this country. We distributed all the books and tracts which we took with us, and two porters' loads besides, which the Rev. Mr. P. sent from Cawnpore at our request to meet us at Hamirpur."

Whether the Allahabad missionaries continued to preach the Gospel in Bundelkhand during the next eleven years, or if they did not, why they were hindered from doing so, the writer cannot tell, as complete reports of that period are not in his possession.

On a tour in Bundelkhand made by Mr. Owen, accompanied by native preachers in December, 1852, the cities of Banda, Hamirpur and Kalpi were visited. In September, 1853, mention is made of a request having been received from an English gentleman at Banda for the establishment of a school at that city under a native Christian teacher. A liberal offer of aid for its support had been made, and the missionaries at Allahabad were considering who, out of their little company of native laborers, was best qualified and could best be spared for this new station. In the following November, a school was established at Banda, with Paul Qaim Khan as head-master, and Melancthon as his assistant. In April 1854, Mr. Owen paid a visit to Banda with the view of making permanent arrangements for a school-house and dwellings for the Christian teachers, and of otherwise strengthening the hands of the native brethren connected with this branch mission. Ten busy days were spent at Banda by the missionary who had been deputed by his brethren at Allahabad to make this visit and to act on their joint behalf as the circumstances in this field might require. He then paid a brief visit to Hamirpur, the head-quarters of the adjoining district of the same name, for the purpose of preaching and of examining a school which the founders desired to make over to the mission. It was Mr. Owen's plan to establish as many schools as possible at the centres of population within reach of Allahabad, in order not only that Christian instruction might systematically be given to hundreds or thousands of pupils who would otherwise grow up without a knowledge of Christ, but also that these schools might furnish students for the mission college at Allahabad, of which he was the principal. At Hamirpur Mr. Owen was joined by two preachers from Fatehpur, and during the eight days spent there many heard the Word from their lips. Mr. Owen returned to Banda from Hamirpur and spent two more days there. He felt thankful to be able to record that there was then in hand for the purpose of providing the buildings needed in Banda the sum of 1,137 rupees. In October of the same year Mr. Owen was found again at Banda. The pupils in the school then numbered 144, and the whole expense of the branch mission was defrayed by English friends who were interested in the work. Subsequently a neat school-house was built by a friend of the mission —F. O. Mayne, Esq., of the Civil Service—with the funds collected for the purpose by Mr. Owen.

But this work so auspiciously begun was rudely terminated by the Sepoy Mutiny of 1857, and was never reinaugurated. Still the missionaries at Allahabad and

Fatehpur never lost sight of the great unoccupied field across the Jumna. From the mission report of 1862-63 we transcribe the following paragraphs :—"Westward of Fatehpur lies an immense district, easy of access, yet almost totally destitute of evangelizing agencies. Crowded with large villages and containing very many people who are willing to hear the truth without prejudice, it seems a promising field for missionary operations. In pursuance of an arrangement by which a considerable part of the expense was borne by the North India Bible Society, a catechist and four Scripture-readers spent about a month of the last year in travelling through Banda and other parts of Bundelkhand, preaching daily in the cities and villages, and circulating the Word of God as widely as possible. The same plan is to be followed during the coming year, and thus will the Word of God be preached as a witness in many places where it would not else be heard for many years to come."

"Mr. Johnson* has, as far as practicable, been sending his native assistants to labor in the city and district of Banda, and we trust the day is not far distant when a permanent agency will again be stationed there."

From the report for the next year we take the following:—"During the month of December, 1863, a preaching tour was made by Mr. Owen of Allahabad in company with Mr. Johnson of Fatehpur, in the province of Bundelkhand as far as Banda and Kalinjar. Two of the native helpers belonging to Fatehpur itinerated in Bundelkhand for nearly five months this year, receiving an allowance from the North India Bible Society to act as colporteurs in distributing the Word of God to the schools. They seem to have done very little of this, however, and to have given their attention almost entire-

* The Rev. W. F. Johnson, D.D., now of Etawah.

ly to preaching, while at the same time they distributed tracts and Gospels among the people. In that region the people seem much more ready to hear the Gospel than in this, and the audiences were much larger, especially in the city of Banda, which has a larger population than Fatehpur. I hope," adds the Rev. Edward H. Sayre, who was then stationed at Fatehpur, " that when the finances of the Board are in a better condition, the mission will allow it to be taken up and occupied as an out-station, by a catechist and a Scripture-reader. The prospect of usefulness there is much greater than here, and only a small outlay would be required."

II.

WORK BEGUN IN GWALIOR, IN THE WEST.

1874.

We have seen how our missionaries at Allahabad and Fatehpur were from the beginning interested in that portion of Bundelkhand which was adjacent to them, and what they sought to do at Banda and elsewhere in that region.

The next portion of the Trans-Jumna region which claims our attention, on account of our missionary undertaking in it, is Gwalior in the west. Gwalior is under native rule, the present rulership being a remnant of a great imperial power, that of the Mahrattas. It is not now an independent State, however, but is subject to the paramount power of Britain. The Mahratta Kingdom of Gwalior, known as that of Scindia, lost a large measure of its independence in 1843, when upon the death of the Maharaja Junkojee Scindia, who died without issue and without having named a successor, serious trouble arose in regard to the regency by which the affairs of the State should be guided and controlled until the boy, then only 8 years old, whom Junkojee's child-widow had adopted as his successor, should attain his majority and be placed upon the throne. Before 1843, indeed, Scindia had not been wholly independent of British control, but at this juncture it was deemed imperative by Lord Ellenborough, the Governor-General, that the Supreme Power should assert its authority more decisively and potentially, not only to put an end to intrigue in the palace at Gwalior, but to gain that ascendency over the over-grown and turbulent army of the Principality, which was in his opinion absolutely essential to the maintenance of British over-lordship in India. The Governor-General's demands at this time not being acceded to, he lost no time in marching an army into the Gwalior territory, and being resisted by the Gwalior troops, two great battles simultaneously ensued, in both of which the British forces were victorious. They however lost in killed and wounded one thousand men. Of the Gwalior forces the slain and disabled in one of the battles alone amounted to three thousand, while as another result of the same engagement no less than fifty-six pieces of ordnance were left upon the field by the Mahrattas. Thus was the Kingdom of Scindia subdued, and it only remained for Queen Victoria's representative on the ground to impose upon the conquered State such restrictions as would render it henceforth impossible for the Gwalior army to menace in any way the safety of the British dominion. It was required of Scindia that of his army of 40,000, 31,000 should be at once disbanded, and the State was allowed to retain only 30 guns, instead of the 200 which it had formerly kept. The British contingent forces, maintained at the expense of the Gwalior State, and garrisoned at the British cantonment of Morar near by, were increased to 10,000. The fortress of Gwalior, one of the strongest in India, was taken possession of by the British, and garrisoned by British soldiers; and it was expressly stipulated by the British Governor-General that henceforth Scindia should act implicitly on the recommendation of the British Political Agent resident at Gwalior, whenever in regard to the affairs of the State he might feel called upon to give him advice.

Though Lord Ellenborough, on account of his excessive fondness for military display, and his neglect of the civil administration in India, was, soon after the occurrence of these events at Gwalior deprived of his office, yet his policy in regard to the army of Scindia was abundantly vindicated when only two years after this it was necessary for the British to engage in war with the Sikhs, and also when fourteen years later the mutiny amongst the sepoys in the British army threatened to drive the British out of India.

The boy, Bhageerut Rao by name, who as the nearest male relative of the Maharaja Junkojee Scindia, had been selected for the Gwalior throne, and whose selection had been approved by the British Governor-General, reached his majority in 1853, and was then placed in power with the royal title of Maharaja Jyajee Scindia. Later on, some account will be given of events in Bundelkhand during the mutiny of 1857-58. It will suffice to say at present that during that trying time the Maharaja Jyajee Scindia, the father of the present ruling Prince, remained faithful to the British Government under circumstances of the most trying character, and doubtless his loyalty, which preserved to him his Kingdom, is to be ascribed in very large measure to the influence of those British Political Agents—Durand, Shakespeare, Sale and Macpherson—who successively resided at Gwalior in the years immediately preceding the mutiny; and also to the counsels of that enlightened Indian Statesman—Dinkar Rao—who was Prime-minister at Gwalior at the time of the mutiny, and in fullest sympathy with the Supreme Government. It was during the reign of the Maharaja Jyajee Scindia that the missionary work of which we are now to speak was commenced at Gwalior.

At the annual meeting of the Furrukhabad Mission in

the autumn of 1873 it was the unanimous feeling of all present that the time had arrived when we ought to send a missionary to Gwalior. From this it might rightly be inferred that in the minds of the members of this mission a feeling of responsibility for the evangelization of the people of Gwalior had been growing for some time previously. This was owing to the fact that the territory of Gwalior bordered upon one of the districts occupied by the Furrukhabad Mission, namely, the district of Etawah.

When it was decided that one of our number should proceed to the capital of Scindia's dominions, both Dr. Brodhead and Dr. Warren promptly volunteered to go to this new field; which shows how important in the estimation of the mission, and particularly in the view of those who coveted the privilege of going to Gwalior, the step we were taking then appeared to be.

For the sake of enabling the reader to understand the situation at Gwalior, it is necessary to point out that Scindia's Capital consists of two cities—one Old Gwalior, as it is called, containing a population of twenty-five or thirty thousand inhabitants; and the other, the Lashkar * or city of the army, containing seventy-five or eighty thousand people. This is the new city which grew up at the army head-quarters when Scindia removed his capital from Ujjain † in Malwa to Gwalior. The Malwa country, in which the former capital was situated, is very fertile, and from its rich fields Scindia derives the greater

* Pronounced Lushkar. The word Lashkar is a Hindi word, meaning the army.

† Ujjain, the old capital of Scindia, with a population of 34,000, is 270 miles south-west of Gwalior. It is one of the mission stations of the Canadian Presbyterian Church. Neemuch, in the Gwalior territory, 120 miles north-west from Ujjain, is another station of the Canadian Presbyterian Mission.

portion of his revenue, whereas much of the country around Gwalior is unfit for cultivation and is sparsely inhabited. The attraction at Gwalior was the great natural fortress, which has been called the "Gibraltar of India." This mass of rock rises precipitously from the plain to the height of more than 300 feet, and is one and a quarter miles in length, and one quarter of a mile in width. The summit of this rock is a level surface, and has upon it, besides extensive buildings for the accommodation of the soldiers garrisoned there, a number of temples of great archæological and architectural interest, one of them probably dating from the tenth century, and another from the eleventh century, as well as the palace built by Raja Man Singh in A.D. 1486-1516. These are solid stone structures, and are ornamented with elaborate carvings. As ancient monuments they are specially cared for by the British Government, the sum of 11,625 rupees having been spent twenty years ago in rescuing them from neglect. The fortress of Gwalior, stretching between the old city and the new one, overlooks both. It is seen from a long distance as one approaches Gwalior, and is a striking feature of the landscape. The two white palaces, adjoining the new city, are large and imposing edifices. One of them, built in modern style, is one of the finest in India. In the same neighborhood and not far from the railway station are a well-appointed guest-house for European visitors, and a capacious and comfortable serai for native travellers. The latter like the former is built of cut stone, and is architecturally a fine structure. It bears the name of "Dufferin." In a suburb of the new city are the Victoria College, recently established, and an extensive hospital founded by the reigning Scindia in memory of his father Jyajee. These are very costly buildings, being constructed of polished stone, and being besides highly ornamented with carvings in oriental fashion.

Five miles from the fortress of Gwalior is Morar, which was for many years previous to 1886 one of the largest British cantonments in the Bengal Presidency. When our missionaries, the Rev. Joseph Warren, D.D., and his wife began to face the situation in the new field to which they had been appointed, they thought it more prudent to settle in Morar, rather than to attempt at the outset to gain a foothold in the immediate vicinity either of old Gwalior or the new city. There was no probability that a house in which to dwell could be obtained in either of these neighborhoods, and it would have been useless at that time to try to secure a building-site on any ground belonging to the Maharaja Scindia or any of his subjects. On British soil the missionaries could settle down quietly, and begin their work without let or hindrance. They found no difficulty in obtaining on rent a suitable residence in Morar, and they were able after a short time to purchase a home of their own, which has ever since been known as the "Mission house." Dr. Warren after being in India from 1839 to 1854, spent 17 years in the United States, and during a part of this period—the years of the civil war—he had served as a chaplain in the U. S. army. At the time of his going to Morar a regiment of Scotch Highlanders was garrisoned there, and they (mostly Presbyterians) were soon after Dr. Warren's arrival deprived of their chaplain. It was at once arranged that Dr. Warren should act as Presbyterian chaplain at Morar, which arrangement not only provided him with an important and congenial sphere of usefulness, but gave him a standing in the British cantonment which was advantageous, and furnished him with pecuniary aid for his missionary work.

In commencing to reach the heathen with the Gospel no opposition whatever was encountered, either in the Morar bazaar, which contained a large native population, or in the city itself; and no difficulties have since arisen in connection with this work. This was doubtless largely due to wise procedure on the part of the pioneer evangelist and his assistants. Imprudence on the part of a missionary to the heathen may cause his work to be seriously hindered or entirely stopped. Commotions unattended with divine blessing are not of the sort which turn the world upside down after the apostolic manner. Such tumults might easily have been stirred up at Gwalior by injudicious action on the part of the Christian preachers. The work of the mission at Morar, which was wholly evangelistic, was carried on unobtrusively until Dr. Warren's death in 1878, and it was not without fruits. A Church was organized, and regular services in connection with it were maintained. The distance from Morar of the main population which it was the mission's object to reach in entering the Gwalior field was and continues to be a great obstacle to the efficient prosecution of the work.

In loneliness of a very exceptional character Mrs. Warren remained at Morar during twenty-two long years, and then went to the United States only for a short sojourn, after being in India continuously for a period of 26 years. She returned to Morar in midsummer 1901 only to die and be laid beside her husband in the English cemetery at that place. At the funeral of the lamented missionary, His Highness the Maharaja Sir Madho Rao Scindia, was not only in attendance, but in preparation for the obsequies every thing had been done at his command which could attest the high esteem in which Mrs. Warren had ever been held by him. One of his gun-carriages drawn by four horses carried the deceased to the grave, and forming a part of the cortege which followed was his own carriage containing himself, his English physician, whose attention to Mrs. Warren during her illness had been unremitting and most kind, and the writer. Mrs. Warren had known the Maharaja from his infancy, and he had been accustomed to speak of her as "mother." In acknowledging the thanks of the mission for the steadfast friendship and unvarying kindness which he had shown to Mrs. Warren he directed the following to be sent to the President of the Mission:—

"JAI BILAS, GWALIOR, 14*th December*, 1901.

DEAR SIR,

I am desired to acknowledge the receipt of your letter dated the 9th instant, with enclosure, and to request you to kindly convey His Highness' thanks to the members of the Furrukhabad Mission for their very kind expression of gratitude.

I may add that the death of Mrs. Warren was a great loss to Gwalior people, and was equally felt by the general public of every age.

I am, yours truly,

A. R. S.,

Private Secretary to

H. H. the Maharaja Scindia."

The Maharaja, according to his desire expressed at the time of Mrs. Warren's death, has placed a stone at her grave, and in accordance with his request mention is made in the inscription upon it that it was erected by him as a mark of his personal esteem.

We are thankful to be able to write that in 1902 other missionaries were sent to be the successors of those who began the work in Gwalior and there laid down their lives. They are the Rev. John Symington, M.D., and his wife, and Mrs. Wyckoff (mother of Mrs. Symington) the widow of the Rev. B. D. Wyckoff, formerly of the Furrukhabad Mission.

III.

WORK BEGUN IN JHANSI, IN CENTRAL BUNDELKHAND.

1873.

We now turn to Jhansi in the heart of Bundela Land. One year before the work in Gwalior was begun, a committee of three was appointed by the mission to visit Jhansi and look over that field with reference to our beginning work there. One member of this committee, the writer of this sketch, was not able to go. The others, Messrs. Ullmann and Kellogg, went, and on their return reported most favorably in regard to the occupation of Jhansi as a station of our mission. Mr. Kellogg, in writing to the Board in New York soon after his return from Jhansi, said, "I am glad to bring a most encouraging report. Throughout the whole country we found the people uncommonly ready to hear the Gospel, and everywhere had very large and attentive congregations. The question of the occupancy of Jhansi by a foreign missionary I need not take up now; it will be laid before the mission. I will only say that it seems to us both an admirable place for a station. I think that, without doubt, our mission will at least direct some one to go down into that region and spend next cold season itinerating."

The outcome of this committee's visit to Jhansi was not the sending of a missionary to this field, as that could not be done at once. The mission felt, however, that something in the direction of occupying this field should be done without delay, and as the Rev. J. F. Ullmann at Etawah was nearer to Central Bundelkhand than any other of our missionaries, he was asked to consider that region as a part of his field, and to do there, by means of his native assistants especially, as much evangelizing as might be found practicable. As the best that could be done under the circumstances, this arrangement was satisfactory to Mr. Ullmann, and so deeply interested was he in the people among whom he had recently been touring, that he determined to send his entire force of helpers into Bundelkhand. The party, of which an ordained minister, the Rev. E. Nabibakhsh, was appointed leader, consisted of six preachers, two colporteurs and one school-teacher. The leader, with the school-teacher and one of the colporteurs, went to Jhansi, and the remaining six were placed in three other large towns, Kalpi, Orai and Koonch—two being appointed to work together in and around each of these centres. At the end of a year the Gospel had been preached not only in the neighborhoods where the preachers were stationed, but also to a considerable extent throughout other parts of Bundelkhand. From Kalpi and Orai tours were made in the district of Jalaun, of which Orai is the head-quarters, lasting altogether forty-seven days. An extensive tour, lasting three months and three days, was made by four of the native assistants who started from Etawah and travelled in the British districts of Jalaun, Jhansi and Lalitpur, and the native States of Sumter and Orcha, visiting two hundred and sixteen towns and villages.

During this year a Brahmin family at Jhansi—husband,

wife and child,—became Christians. The man was highly respected in that city as priest of one of the principal temples there. He first bought a New Testament from one of the preachers, and from reading that, and by means of the instruction which he received, was led to reject Hinduism and embrace Christianity. It was a catechist from the lowest caste of the Hindus who was the instructor of this man, and thus was shown how the Lord honors those whom the world despises. The people of Jhansi were amazed at this conversion, and said to the catechist, "There must be some magic in your books, which turned our priest's head. You have taken one of our best men, who was made priest of that temple of our goddess by our Maharaja, and you have made him a Christian." To this the catechist replied, "If your great goddess Lakshmi had any power, she would have prevented her priest from leaving her, but you see, our Lord Jesus Christ by his almighty power laid hold of her priest, and drew him to himself, turning him who was a (Devidás (servant of the goddess) into a Prabhudás servant of the Lord)." The name Prabhudás was chosen by the convert himself when he was baptized.

This work in Bundelkhand, superintended from Etawah, was carried on for three years, when partly on account of the difficulty of directing and overseeing it from such a distance, and for other reasons also, it was found necessary to withdraw the workers from that field.

Not till the autumn of 1885 did the mission see its way to taking up its work again in Central Bundelkhand. At the annual meeting of the mission, which then took place, this field was again talked of, and subsequently a committee of four was appointed to visit Jhansi and report upon the advisability or otherwise of its being made a mission station to be occupied by a missionary.

The immediate cause of this revival of interest in Jhansi was the news which had reached us through Mrs. Warren at Morar, that the British garrison was to be withdrawn from Gwalior, that Morar was to be abandoned as a British cantonment, and that the fortress of Gwalior was to be restored to Scindia. The British garrison at Jhansi was to be increased, and the fort and city of Jhansi, which belonged to Scindia, were to become British possessions. These changes, which were to be effected within a few months, would be alike satisfactory to the British Government and to Scindia, as the need no longer existed of maintaining the British contingent force at Morar. Since 1843 the British had held the great fortress which overlooked Scindia's capital and cantonment, and this state of things had continued notwithstanding the fact that the Maharaja, Jyajee Scindia, on account of his loyalty to the British Government and his military experience, had been made an Honorary Major-General of the British Army in India. The rendition of this fortress had been to Scindia, as might be supposed, an object of great desire. Equally satisfactory to the British was it to obtain the fort and city of Jhansi in exchange for what they were entirely ready to relinquish at Gwalior; for the situation of the British residents at Jhansi, both civil and military, was exceedingly unpleasant and otherwise undesirable, as they were obliged to be quartered in close proximity to Scindia's city, within which was the strong fort, garrisoned by Gwalior State troops.

The native Principality of Jhansi, including the capital city and a large territory surrounding it had lapsed to the British in 1853, when the reigning Prince had died without issue, and his adoption of a youth distantly related to him to be his successor was disallowed; but in 1861 the city of Jhansi with a large portion of territory on one side of it had been ceded to Scindia, leaving the territory, up to the city wall on the other side, to the British.

It was because the Indian Midland Railway, opening up this part of Central India, and having its head-quarters at Jhansi, where four lines would converge, would soon be completed, that the British forces, no longer needed at Morar as a strategic point, could be withdrawn and placed with greater advantage at Jhansi and elsewhere.

Under the new conditions at Gwalior it was doubtful whether our mission would be allowed to remain there. Hence the importance of our seeking to gain at Jhansi a position which might compensate us for the loss we might be obliged to sustain at Gwalior. Besides, Jhansi in itself was to become one of the most desirable locations in Central India as a centre for missionary operations.

IV.

CHARACTERISTICS OF BUNDELKHAND AND ITS PEOPLE.

Anticipating the account to be given of the visit to Jhansi of the mission's committee appointed near the end of 1885, it will be well to acquaint the reader somewhat with the characteristics of Bundelkhand and its people, and the political history of the district which became, as the result of the committee's recommendation a part of the Furrukhabad Mission field.

It is interesting to note in passing that Ptolemy, who completed his great work on geography in A.D. 151, was not ignorant of the region now known as Bundelkhand, for he speaks of the famous rock Kalinjar under the name of Kanagara.

The appearance of the greater part of the country bearing the name of Bundelkhand is very different from the uniformly level plain of the adjoining Doab, in which most of the stations of the Furrukhabad Mission are situated. The landscape is diversified with hills which in the middle portion of this region not unfrequently rise like pyramids abruptly from the plain, "suggesting," as has been said, "the idea of rocky islands rearing themselves out of the sea"; then there are ranges of hills intersecting the plain, running for the most part from the south toward the north-east, and extending sometimes for long distances; while in the south-eastern and south-western parts rise the higher Bindachal mountains, which are a part of the Vindya system of Central India. Much of the land is rocky and unfit for cultivation. In those tracts where good soil is found, the variety of green fields or ripening harvests, and hills rising here and there in the midst of them, is very pleasing to the eye. Some of the hills are for the most part bare rocks, often presenting to the view the most fantastic shapes, while others, covered with a great variety of trees and verdure, are exquisitely picturesque. Many of the hills are crowned with ruined forts, which once afforded refuge and defense to bands of robbers with which the country was infested. Some of these forts were occupied as residences by robber chieftains. The villages in the neighborhood of these forts belonged to these chiefs, and every male adult was compelled to declare himself as attached to some marauding leader in his village. All were practised in the use of weapons of warfare, and no one left his home without being suitably armed, for the taking of life on the highway was no uncommon occurrence. Abul Fazl, the favorite minister of the Emperor Akbar, when passing through Bundelkhand on his way from the Deccan to Delhi, was waylaid and murdered by the notorious free-booter, Bir Singh Deo, who subsequently became one of the most famous of the line of Bundela kings. His capital was at Orcha, within a few miles of the place where the city of Jhansi was afterwards founded. On account of the warlike and predatory character of the inhabitants of Bundelkhand at that time, the Mahomedan Emperors of Delhi, to whom they owed a nominal allegiance, were never able to bring them under entire subjection, and as a consequence they could collect from them but comparatively little tribute. Bundelkhand as it was in the time of the Bundela kings has been truly described as a land sacred to brigandism. As a matter of course under such conditions agriculture languished, and commerce was beset with difficulties and risks which rendered it well nigh prohibitive, for property, especially that which was moveable, was utterly insecure. As late as the year 1872, the Agent of the British Governor-General, who had recently made a tour in the vicinity of the old capital of the Bundela Chiefs, wrote, "I could not fail to observe in passing through Orcha, that this country of rocks, forest-covered wastes and forts is populated by thousands, who but for the British prestige would make the old hills ring again with their war cries." Still more recently bands of dacoits in this same region have been hunted down and shot, or if captured have been sent into exile. The masses of the people, who are peaceable cultivators of the soil, are most thankful to Government for being delivered from the depredations and cruelties committed by such villainous plunderers.

In the districts of Hamirpur and Jhansi are numerous artificial lakes, some of them several miles in circumference, which were formed by damming up small streams, whose beds are dry or nearly dry in the hot weather, but which in the rainy season are filled with water. The stone embankments of some of these lakes are very extensive, and their structure is elaborate, showing that they were built at enormous expense. The great embankment of the beautiful lake and the adjoining castle at Barwa Sagar, twelve miles from Jhansi, were begun by one of the Bundela Kings in 1705, and completed in 1737.

On account of the large amount of waste land in Bundelkhand the population is not so dense as in the more fertile parts of Central India. Famines, due to the failure of rain, have occurred here more frequently than elsewhere in this part of India, but so much has been done by the Government for the salvation of life and the relief of suffering when famines have occurred, that the villagers have good reason to be grateful and loyal to their present rulers, as indeed they appear to be.

In Bundelkhand are found a great number of native States, some of them quite insignificant in size, and others of considerable importance both territorially and politically, which, while nominally independent, are under British protection and control. That part of Bundelkhand in which Jhansi lies, is remarkable for the intermixture of territory owned by native Chiefs with that which belongs to the Supreme Government. Every road which connects Jhansi with some other portion of British territory passes through one or more native States, and in passing from one part of the Jhansi district to another, it is frequently necessary to cross over a strip of country belonging to some native Chief. All these roads, however, belong to the British Government, and in our intercourse with the people as missionaries, it is of little consequence whether we know or do not know to whom a certain village belongs.

Before the Indian Midland Railway was built, Jhansi was one of the most out-of-the-way places in India. In fact during the rainy season it was sometimes almost entirely cut off from communication with other parts of the country by swollen rivers; but that state of things exists no more. From being in an exceptionally isolated position, its connections with all parts of India have, through the different lines of railway centring here become exceptionally convenient.

Although Bundelkhand received its name from its

early conquerors, the Bundelas, the Bundela clan at the time of its ascendency in Central India seems not to have been a very large one, and the descendants of this once powerful dynasty are now not numerous in Bundelkhand. The usual mixture of Indian nationalities, tribes and castes found in the regions adjacent to Bundelkhand exists here also at the present time. The Mahomedan element of the population is neither large nor influential. The influence of Hinduism is predominant, but among the Hindus of Bundelkhand bigotry and caste prejudice are not as strong as among the same classes in other districts occupied by our missionaries.

V.

THE FOUNDING OF JHANSI, AND THE POLITICAL HISTORY OF THE PRINCIPALITY.*

The fort of Jhansi was built by the Bundela Chief, Bir Singh Deo, about two hundred and seventy-five years ago. The rock on which it is built was the site of a small village called Balwantnagar (strong town). The founding of the city of Jhansi was commenced about one hundred and sixty years ago, but the city was named about a century before it was built. The origin of the name is explained by the people of Orcha on this wise :—They relate that the Raja of Jaitpur was on a visit to Bir Singh Deo, and when one day both were sitting on the roof of the palace at Orcha, the latter, pointing in the direction of his new fort in the distance (about six miles off), asked his guest if he could see it. Shading his eyes with his hand, and looking intently in the direction indicated, the Jaitpur Raja replied, "Jháin-sí," meaning "shadow-like," by which he intended that he could see it indistinctly; and through this incident the city which afterwards grew up around the fort came to be named Jhansi.

The city of Jhansi was founded as the capital of a Mahratta Principality. In the early decades of the eighteenth century two great rival powers came into con-

* That is, up to the time of its annexation by the British Governor-General, Lord Dalhousie.

THE FORT OF JHANSI.

flict in Central India. They were the Mahomedan Moguls, having their capital at Delhi, and the Mahrattas (a numerous and warlike race of Hindus), whose capital was at Poona in the Deccan, eighty miles south-east of Bombay. The Delhi Emperors were seeking to establish their supremacy in Bundelkhand, where they had hitherto held but a nominal sway. The Mahrattas were endeavoring by every possible means to extend their dominion toward the north-east, their ultimate aim being the overthrow of the Musalman Empire, and to further this end they were anxious to obtain the control of Bundelkhand, for the purpose of opening up a safe highway between the Mahratta country and the Ganges-Jumna Doab. The Bundela Chiefs in Central India were in a situation strikingly similar to that of the Kings of Judah and Israel, when they had to be on their guard against invasions of the Assyrian hosts from the north-east, and incursions of the Egyptian armies from the south-west.

Chhatarsal, one of he greatest of the Bundela Chiefs, had been exceedingly successful at this same period not only in his encounters with various Mahomedan leaders, but also in subjecting to his rule the minor Bundela Chiefs, who from time to time impugned his advancing authority; and his active and aggressive leadership had resulted in greatly extending his dominion. In fact his success in warfare had rendered insecure the position to which his superior prowess had exalted him. For, although on the accession of Bahadur Shah as Emperor at Delhi, he had been received at Court as a loyal feudatory, and had been confirmed in the possession of all his recently conquered territories, yet he could not feel safe from Mahomedan invasions. And good reason had he to fear for his safety. He was very soon after attacked by a Mahomedan leader, who falling suddenly upon his forces defeated them, and spread devastation far and wide in Bundelkhand.

Under these circumstances it seemed to him that the wisest course he could follow would be to call in the aid of the Mahrattas, who under the first Peshwa, Baji Rao, were at that time advancing slowly but steadily through Khandesh and Malwa towards Bundelkhand. This step, as the result showed, proved to be but a choice between two evils. The Mahratta Peshwa gladly availed himself of an opportunity to obtain sooner than he had hoped a foothold in the territory which then owed allegiance to Chhatarsal, by coming to the aid of this Prince in his time of need. The combined Mahratta and Bundela forces quickly hemmed in the Mahomedan invader, who soon became so far reduced that he was obliged to capitulate and retire from the field where he had been so victorious. Chhatarsal, when he had regained his possessions, ceded a portion of his territory to the Peshwa as a reward for his assistance, and he subsequently bequeathed to him one-third of his dominions on the condition that his heirs and successors should be maintained by the Peshwa in the possession of the remainder. The area bequeathed to the Peshwa included the fort which the Bundela Chief, Bir Singh Deo, had built on the site which was afterwards included in the precincts of the city of Jhansi.

Thus about the year 1734 was gained the first territorial acquisition of the Mahrattas in Bundelkhand. Other more important acquisitions were soon made by the second Peshwa. The first Peshwa died in 1740, when his son, Balaji Baji Rao, succeeded to the Mahratta throne. The new Peshwa, apparently in utter disregard of the agreement which his father had entered into with Chhatarsal, undertook fresh military operations in 1742, for the purpose of extending his dominion in Bundelkhand. By his direction a strong force, commanded by an experienced Mahratta general, named Naru Sankar, was sent to attack Orcha, the Bundela capital, which was easily reduced to subjection, the Raja making but slight resistance, knowing that it was useless for him to oppose so powerful a foe. The Mahratta general determined to make the overthrow of Orcha complete, and the flourishing city when given up to him soon became a scene of desolation. In the partitioning of the possessions of the Orcha State the Raja was permitted to retain a minor portion of his territory, and he set up a new capital at Tehri, fifty miles south of Orcha, where his successors have since ruled. By the fall of the old Bundela capital the Peshwa acquired the major portion of the lands belonging to the Orcha State, including most of the tract which afterwards constituted the Mahratta Principality of Jhansi, and which eventually became a possession of the British.

Over the Peshwa's newly acquired domain in Bundelkhand Naru Sankar was appointed the first governor, and he chose as his head-quarters the fort which Bir Singh Deo had built at Balwantnagar. This he considerably enlarged, while at the same time he began to found the present city of Jhansi, by compelling the inhabitants of other towns, those of Orcha in particular, to leave their homes and settle in it, as well as by encouraging Mahrattas to come and take up their residence there. Under him Jhansi soon became an important city, and it maintained its prosperity under successive governors.

An Englishman who visited the place in 1792 described it thus:—" It is frequented by caravans from the Deccan, which go to Furrukhabad and the other cities of the Doab. Hence an afflux of wealth, which is augmented by a considerable trade in the cloths of Chanderi, and by the manufacture of bows, arrows and spears, the principal weapons of the Bundela tribes."

The city wall was not built until the years between 1796 and 1814. It was erected during the governorship of Sheo Rao Bhao, and has not been much altered since then. It is three miles and five furlongs in extent. Its height varies from eighteen to twenty-seven feet, and its width from six to twelve feet. It is solidly constructed of granite stones and cement, the former having been quarried from the adjacent hills. Bastions upon which cannon can be mounted, situated at suitable points, form parts of the wall. Connected with the wall on the west side are the ramparts of the fort. Entrance to the city was afforded by ten principal gates and eight smaller ones, all of which for the purpose of ensuring the safety of the inhabitants from danger from without were closed at night. All of these gateways except three are still used. Of those which are in use, some remain open day and night, while others are regularly closed some time after nightfall as of old. In these days no purpose is served by closing at night the gates of a walled city in India. But if any object were to be gained by it, that object would fail of accomplishment if some of the gates were closed, while others were left open. This is but one of innumerable cases everywhere and constantly in evidence in this land, showing the inveterate force and recognized authority of long established custom upon the minds of the people of India. Especially do we observe this, and have continual occasion to lament it, in religious matters. As long as the wall of a city is regarded as a thing of utility, it must needs be kept in repair. And likewise the more

ONE OF THE ENTRANCES TO JHANSI.

devoted adherents of a decaying religion feel it necessary to restore and buttress it to the utmost of their ability. The ancient wall of Hinduism has in these modern times shown marked signs of weakness: hence the efforts which its upholders are with so much assiduity putting forth to repair it.

During seventy-five years Jhansi continued to be ruled by governors appointed from time to time by the Peshwa. But when the Peshwa's power began to wane, as was the case toward the end of the eighteenth century, the governors at Jhansi ruled more like independent chiefs than as viceroys. This was the state of things at the time when the British appeared upon the scene in Bundelkhand. Sheo Rao Bhao, whose term of office as governor extended over a period of twenty years, was in power at the advent of the British, and by grant dated February 4, 1804, was promised their protection under certain conditions, though he was still held to be nominally subject to the authority of the Peshwa. This arrangement was confirmed by treaty in October 1806.

How at this early period the British came to be in Bundelkhand must now be told. In the wonderful evolution of events under Divine Providence it occurred that the Mahrattas, who at the solicitation of Chhatarsal had interfered on his behalf against a Mahomedan invader, and had as a reward for their services obtained a portion of territory from the Bundela Chief, and from this beginning had soon attained to the sovereignty of Bundelkhand, were in their turn the means of opening to the British the door to political supremacy in this part of Central India. It came about on this wise:—On account of bitter enmities and irreconcilable dissensions among the Mahratta Chiefs the time when peace could again be established between them seemed forever to have passed. Frequent conflicts were occurring between the Peshwa and his powerful lieutenants, Holkar and Scindia, as well as between the latter potentates, whose rivalries were incessant. In 1802 the Peshwa was driven from his capital by Holkar, and took refuge in British territory. In his discomfiture he was led to enter into negotiations with the British, which issued in the treaty of Bassein, signed on December 31, 1802, whereby the British undertook to restore him to his throne at Poona, on condition of his entering into alliance with them and receiving at his capital a British military force sufficient to ensure his safety, the Peshwa at the same time agreeing to cede to the British a portion of territory, the revenue of which amounted to 2,600,000 rupees, for the maintenance of this force. Accordingly an army was organized under General Arthur Wellesley (afterwards the Duke of Wellington) for the purpose of recovering the Mahratta capital for the Peshwa. Poona was taken on April 20, 1803 without the firing of a single shot, Holkar deeming it the part of wisdom for him to retreat before the advancing British force, and on May 13th the Peshwa was again established in his royal palace, where as a protected sovereign he might have ended his days in peace, but ere long he became the centre of intrigue against his protectors, and before fifteen years had passed an attempt was made by a powerful Mahratta force to eject the British from their capital. They were defeated, however, and the Peshwa fled precipitately from his capital never again to return. The outcome of this perfidy on the part of Baji Rao was his dethronement and the annexation of the greater part of his dominions. Thus did the British gain the virtual supremacy in all the country ruled by the Mahratta Chiefs, though Holkar and Scindia had yet to be subdued.

During the time that General Wellesley was operating in the Deccan (for much still remained to be accomplished there), the British Commander-in-Chief, General Lake, undertook the subjugation first of Scindia, and afterwards of Holkar, and succeeded in effectually breaking the power of these Chiefs in Central India and in the North, where henceforth the British remained in paramount authority. The "Middle Land," as that country was formerly called which afterwards became known under the British as the North-West Provinces, came at that time under British rule. It fell to the lot of the successors of Lord Wellesley—Lord Minto and the Marquess of Hastings—to pacificate these territories which had been brought under British control, and especially to the latter, who himself took the field as Commander-in-Chief of the British forces, was due the credit of freeing from hordes of armed ruffians the whole region which had long suffered from anarchy and the most cruel spoliation. The magnitude of this undertaking may be inferred from the fact that Lord Hastings assembled for the purpose the strongest British army which up to that time had been seen in India, numbering one hundred and twenty thousand men. Lord Hastings, like Lord Cornwallis, who had been Governor-General of India before him, had gone through the American war before coming to this part of the world.

A few months before the outbreak against the British at Poona in 1817 the Peshwa had ceded to the British East India Company his claim of sovereignty in Bundelkhand, and in consequence of this it had become necessary for the British to make fresh arrangements with those who were in authority there, including the Mahratta Chief at Jhansi. The Mahratta Governor, Sheo Rao Bhao, had died in 1814, and had bequeathed his rights to his grandson, Ram Chand Rao. The British East India Company by treaty, dated November 18, 1817, acknowledged the succession of Ram Chand Rao, his heirs and successors, as hereditary rulers.

Thus did a descendant of one who had been a servant of a king become a reigning Prince, and the first of a line of hereditary Princes. And thus through various vicissitudes in days gone by, many heads of royal houses in India obtained their prerogatives as independent chiefs; and at the present time their descendants enjoy such hereditary titles as Raja or Maharaja, Gaekwar, Nizam or Nawab, or whatever it may be. At one time, as Meredith Townsend has well said, "the whole continent (of India) was open as a prize to the strong. A brigand, for Sivaji (the greatest of the Mahratta kings) was no better, became a mighty sovereign. A herdsman built a monarchy in Baroda. A body-servant (slipper-bearer) founded the dynasty of Scindia. A corporal cut his way to the independent crown of Mysore. The first Nizam was only an officer of the Emperor. Runjeet Singh's father was what Europeans would call a prefect." The writer remembers that when visiting Jeypore, he was introduced to the Prime-minister of that State in his magnificent drawing-room, and that his friend after the interview with that high functionary remarked concerning him that he had once been a camel-driver. Many of those who rose to high places in the India of former times were men of no ordinary ability, and doubtless it is true that many of those who in these modern times come to the front in this land owe their advancement largely, if not entirely, to their individual merits.

An important service rendered to the British East India Company by Ram Chand Rao, which was the occasion of the bestowment upon him of a royal title, deserves mention. In 1825 the siege of Bhurtpore was in progress under Lord Combermere, in consequence of which great excitement prevailed throughout Central India. During this disturbed state of affairs, a rebel chief, named Nana Pundit, had collected a considerable force, and was threatening an attack upon the British town of Kalpi. On being apprised of this, the British Political Agent, Mr. Ainslie, sent a request to the Jhansi Chief for aid, and Ram Chand Rao immediately despatched four hundred cavalry, one thousand infantry and some artillerymen with two guns. These arrived in time to prevent Kalpi from being captured by the rebels, and a future substantial result of this prompt action in aid of the British was that confidence in the success of the British cause was restored among the people of that region. This important military service rendered to the British East India Company was expressly referred to in the highest terms of commendation and gratitude by the Governor-General, Lord William Bentinck, at a great durbar held in the palace at Jhansi on the 19th December, 1832; on which occasion the title of Raja was conferred upon the ruler of Jhansi. At this same time the Jhansi Chief asked and obtained permission to have the British flag carried before him as a token of his loyalty, and to append to the title just bestowed upon him the appellation—" Devoted servant of the glorious King of England." Thenceforth amongst the insignia of his royal house was treasured a Union Jack of silk, presented to him by the British Governor-General.

The story of the Jhansi Government under the Rajas is short, and it is for the most part one of misrule and consequent deterioration. Their Government came to an end in twenty-one years. Raja Ram Chand Rao's revenues, owing to mismanagement, became greatly diminished, and the weakness of his administration was shown by the fact that the neighboring landlords could at their will overrun his territory and plunder his villages. Not unfrequently were whole villages burned, causing their inhabitants to be totally ruined. Ram Chand Rao, the first Raja of Jhansi, died without issue in 1835, and was succeeded by his uncle Ragonath Rao, second son of Sheo Rao Bhao. From maladministration his revenues declined, and becoming deeply in debt through extravagance and debauchery he was obliged to mortgage some of his villages to the Gwalior and Orcha States. He died without issue in 1838, his rule having been made unquiet by opposition shown to him professedly on the ground of his being a leper. He was succeeded by his brother Gangadhar Rao, third son of Sheo Rao Bhao. The Government of the State was not however handed over to him at once, the British Governor-General deeming it advisable on account of the distracted state of the Principality that his Agent in Bundelkhand should assume the administration temporarily. The revenues under British management were in a single year considerably more than doubled. In 1842 the state of the country was such that it seemed judicious to place the Government in the hands of the legitimate heir to the Principality. The administration of Gangadhar Rao was an improvement on that of his predecessors. He gave proof of his taking a personal interest in his estate by giving attention in some degree to matters of public benefit, and was therefore popular as a ruler. He died childless in November 1853, and there was no male heir to succeed him. He was the last of the Mahrattas who held the reins of Government in Jhansi.

On the death of this Chief it devolved upon Lord

Dalhousie, who was then the British Governor-General in India, to decide a very grave question in regard to the Jhansi Principality. Gangadhar Rao on the day before his death had adopted as his successor a youth distantly related to him, and the question to be settled was whether in right, and in justice to all the interests involved in the case, this adoption should be sanctioned by the Supreme Government. The decision arrived at by the British East India Company's most able Representative was that the adoption could not be allowed to stand, and consequently that the Jhansi State lapsed to the Company.

VI.

THE MUTINY IN JHANSI, AND THE REVENGE OF THE RANI LAKSHMI BAI.

Lakshmi Bai, the widow of the deceased Raja, famous as the Rani of Jhansi, was greatly incensed at the rejection by Lord Dalhousie and his Council of what she regarded as an indisputable right, and she most strenuously protested that the action of the British Government in disallowing the claim which she had urged on behalf of the lad whom her husband had adopted, thereby erasing Jhansi from the list of native States, was unjust and indefensible. The terms of the treaty which the British East India Company made with Ram Chand Rao at the time when the title of Raja of Jhansi was conferred upon him, constituted his heirs and successors hereditary rulers of the territory governed by the Peshwa's viceroys since the founding of Jhansi as a Mahratta Principality; and the Rani's contention, which she put forward in her petition to the British Governor-General, was that the original Persian terms used in the treaty, and interpreted heirs and successors, meant not merely heirs of the body or collateral heirs, but successors in general, and properly implied that any party whom the Raja adopted as his son, to perform the funeral rites over his body, necessary according to Hindu law to insure beatitude in a future world, would be acknowledged by the British Government as his successor, and as one through whom the name and interests of the family might be preserved.

The Rani's protestations, however, were of no avail. The Governor-General had fully considered the case in all its aspects, and his decision could not be revoked. None of Lord Dalhousie's acts gave to the hostile critics of his policy (and there were many such critics both out of India and in it) greater offence than the annexation of Jhansi. But those whose sympathies were with the Princess, whose claim had been set aside, were not able to take so broad and far-reaching a view of this subject as had been taken by the British Statesman, who not only felt most deeply his responsibility for the welfare of the people of Jhansi, but who looked most carefully at the legal features of the case both from the standpoint of the claimant to the rulership of the State and from that of the Over-lord. There can be no doubt that Lord Dalhousie had a technical and absolute right to do what he did, but at the same time there is room for a difference of opinion in regard to the political wisdom of his action. Judged from the immediate results which followed from the course which he pursued, his policy was disastrous, but how can one who has regard to the benefits of a beneficent Government now enjoyed by the inhabitants of this part of India rightly blame Lord Dalhousie for doing what he considered at the time to be right and for the best interests of those on whose behalf he was called to act? Of Lord Dalhousie's annexations that one which was perhaps more severely criticised than any other, is, if I mistake not, likely to be regarded with less and less disfavor, as the standpoint from which it shall be viewed shall grow more and more distant by lapse of time.

We cannot, however, blame the Rani for taking the

view of the case which she did, as Lord Dalhousie's decision in reference to Jhansi could not but seem to her an act of the grossest injustice. She looked upon the rejection of her claim as a personal dethronement, for had the petition which she pressed upon the Governor-General been granted, she would in all probability have been allowed to act as Regent until the boy chosen by the Raja to be his successor should become of age, and even after the installation of the new Raja she would have remained in a position of commanding influence. Her deprivation could not therefore but seem to her to be very great.

The Rani felt exceedingly indignant on account of the smallness of the annuity, £6,000, which had been assigned to her by the British authorities, and at first she refused it. Afterwards, however, she consented to accept it. She was still further aggrieved because after the property which had belonged to her husband, valued at 1,000,000 rupees, had been made over to her by the British Government, the Lieutenant-Governor directed that a sum of money sufficient to liquidate her husband's debts should be deducted from her annual allowance. Against this the Rani earnestly protested, and Sir Robert Hamilton, the Governor-General's Agent in Central India, urged on Mr. Colvin the advisability of pursuing a generous policy, but the Lieutenant-Governor's action was in keeping with the careless indifference with which the Supreme Government regarded the Rani's anger and her remonstrances. Is it any wonder that she brooded over her wrongs, and was eager to avenge them?

Again, she and her people felt that insult was being added to injury by the slaughter of kine (sacred in the estimation of Hindus), which was as a matter of course introduced by the British into their newly acquired territory. Besides, the wholesome regulations in regard to sanitation, inaugurated by the new rulers, were also extremely irritating to many who objected to any restrictions upon their practices even when the public health was endangered.

For a time the Rani took no pains to conceal from the British the bitter resentment and deadly hatred which she cherished towards them, for she could not but regard them as intruders and usurpers, but at length she adopted the policy of remaining reticent in their presence regarding the wrongs which she felt herself and her people to be enduring, resolved to bide patiently her time for revenge. She had not long to wait, for in the short space of three and a half years her opportunity arrived. During the greater part of this period, as far as appearances went, she was on terms of good-will with the British officers at Jhansi, for as an Oriental, even when fierce wrath burned within her, she was able to set bounds to her temper and even to exhibit friendliness, when to do this required her to put an immense restraint upon her real feeling. Among her own people, however, she did not remain silent nor inactive, but on the contrary put forth every effort to fan the fire of hatred towards the British which glowed in their hearts. To arouse them to the highest pitch of feeling she needed only to assert, as she was in the habit of doing, that the foreigners were seeking to destroy their religion.

The Rani, possessed of a powerful intellect and masculine energy, and fired with indomitable resolution and blood-thirsty vindictiveness, proved to be a woman whom it was dangerous to provoke. She was, moreover, full of the fire of youth, her age probably not exceeding five and twenty years. She was comely in person and tall of stature, and was not backward to show herself to the multitude. She was in fact in all respects fitted to be another Joan of Arc, which indeed she did become.

The following record of occurrences at Jhansi in the summer of 1857 is made after collating and amalgamating the accounts given by Sir John W. Kaye and Col. Malleson in their histories of the Indian Mutiny. It was found that these accounts were mutually supplementary, and a comparison of their statements has been of service in enabling the writer to eliminate a few errors. In some instances the language of the above authors has been retained.

To enable the reader to understand the situation of the British at Jhansi, it is necessary to state that the "Civil Station", as that quarter is called where the Civil officers and other Europeans reside, is immediately outside the city wall toward the south. The bungalows occupied by Capt. Alexander Skene, who was the political and administrative officer in this part of Bundelkhand, and of Capt. F. D. Gordon, who was the magistrate of the Jhansi district, were within ten minutes drive of the fort and palace inside the native city. The officers and clerks (Europeans) in Government offices, numbered in all twenty-two, while the whole number of British and Eurasian residents in the "Civil Station" was sixty, comprising twenty-six men, fifteen women and nineteen children. Beyond the "Civil Station" is situated the British Cantonment. The garrison at the time of the mutiny in Jhansi in 1857 consisted of a wing of the Twelfth Bengal Native Infantry, comprising five companies, the head-quarters and right wing of the Fourteenth Irregular Cavalry and a detachment of Foot Artillery. The garrison was commanded by Capt. Dunlop of the Twelfth Native Infantry. The other British officers were Lieut. Taylor of the Twelfth Native

Infantry, Lieut. Campbell of the Fourteenth Irregular Cavalry, Quarter-master Sergeant Newton, who had with him his wife and two children, and Conductor Reilly. Of the British there were in the Cantonment but these eight souls. Within the Cantonment and very near to the "Civil Station" is a walled enclosure which was occupied by the Artillery, and contained the magazine and treasure-chest. This because built in the form of a star was called the "star fort."

Early in 1857 signs of the great Sepoy Mutiny, which was about to break out and severely test the resources of the British Government, began to appear in Bengal and in the North. The news of disaffection in the native regiments was spread far and wide, and when it reached the ears of the deposed Rani of Jhansi, it was hailed by her with the greatest joy. On the 10th of May occurred the rising in the Cantonment of Meerut, and this was followed on the next day by the outbreak at Delhi. Great alarm was created in most places in North and Central India as the tidings of these occurrences were received, and the consternation increased as outbreaks in other places followed. It was strange that in Jhansi, which had been such a hot-bed of discontent, little or no fear from the sepoys was apprehended by the British officers either in the Civil Station or the Cantonment. They remained strangely unapprehensive of danger, and ignorant of what was taking place in their very midst.

The Rani, whose hopes for the future were brightened by the news received from Meerut and Delhi, had at once hurried off from the doors of her palace confidential messengers towards the sepoy barracks, and these brought back reports corresponding to her expectations. Thus her intrigue with the troops in the British garrison began. With true Mahratta cunning she sought to lull the British officers of the garrison and district into a feeling of security, while plotting for their overthrow. She gained her end by pretending that she was in danger from the enemies of the British, thus intimating that her interests and safety were bound up with the British cause. In Capt. Skene, through whom chiefly her designs were prosecuted, she found pliable material to work upon. So impressed was he with her sincerity and loyalty to the British, that he readily acceded to her request for permission to enlist a body of armed men for her own protection from any attack of the sepoys! She did indeed desire to make provision for her own defence, but her real object was successfully disguised. No sooner had she obtained permission to provide for her own safety than she began to rally round her the old soldiers of the State, and unobserved by the British officers, she had the heavy guns unearthed which had been buried at the time of her husband's death. While all this busy preparation was being made for the annihilation of those whom she was professing to regard as her friends, Capt. Skene was reporting to the Lieutenant-Governor at Agra his entire satisfaction with the state of things at Jhansi. As late as the 18th of May he wrote, "I do not think there is any cause for alarm about this neighborhood. The troops here continue staunch, and express their unbounded abhorrence of the atrocities committed at Meerut and Delhi. . . . . I am going on the principle of showing perfect confidence, and I am quite sure I am right." On the 30th of May he wrote, "All continues quiet here, and the troops staunch, but there is of course a great feeling of uneasiness among the moneyed men of the town, and the Thakurs (descendants of Bundela free-booters) who have never been well-affected towards any government, are beginning, it is

THE STAR FORT.

said, to talk of doing something. All will settle down here, I feel perfectly certain, on receipt of intelligence of success." Again on the 3rd of June, "We are all safe here as yet."

Capt. Dunlop and his fellow-officers of the garrison were similarly trustful. The commandant placed special trust in his Irregular Cavalry. The bungalows of some British officials at Jhansi had been burned, but such an occurrence, which was the invariable precursor of a rising of the sepoys, did not disturb Skene and Dunlop. A fire which occurred on June 1st was attributed to accident. At last when unmistakable signs of an outbreak appeared on the 5th of June, the civilians thought it prudent to betake themselves to the fort in the city.

On that day a company of the Twelfth Native Infantry, led by a native sergeant, and cheered on by the native gunners of the battery, marched into the star fort and announced their intention to hold it as their own. On hearing of this Capt. Dunlop rushed to the parade ground, accompanied by his officers. The remaining four companies professed to be highly indignant at the conduct of their insubordinate comrades who had acted so audaciously, and they and the cavalry troops declared emphatically that they would stand by their officers. On parade the next morning they repeated their protestations of loyalty. Capt. Dunlop began to prepare measures for bringing the revolted company to reason, or to subdue them in case they would not yield to persuasion, and while so engaged he was visited by Captains Skene and Gordon from the fort. After the interview with Dunlop, Skene returned at once to the fort, but Gordon breakfasted in his own bungalow, and before returning to the fort, wrote letters to the Tehri and Datia Rajas and to the Rao of Gursarai for assistance. No replies were received from any of these Chiefs, although they were near at hand, and could easily have responded to the call for help. Capt. Dunlop wrote some letters after Skene and Gordon left him, and posted them himself. On his way back from the post-office he was shot by his own men. About this time the Rani, escorted by her new levies, and accompanied by a crowd of people, among whom were her chief adherents, with two banners borne aloft, went in procession from the palace to the Cantonment. After she and the rabble which accompanied her had issued from the Saiyar gate (the principal gate of the city), a Mahomedan Mulla, named Ahsan Ali, called all true believers to prayers. This was the prearranged signal for the rising of the troops in the Cantonment, and accordingly a ready response was given to it. First the mutineers sought to destroy the officers who were still in the Cantonment, and they succeeded in putting all to death except two. One of these, according to one account, was Lieut. Taylor and according to another, was Lieut. Campbell, who when fired upon was severely wounded, but nevertheless was able to escape on horseback to the fort. The other was Conductor Reilly, who escaped to a neighboring town, and from there eventually made his way to a place of safety. Lieut. Turnbull of the survey department was in the Cantonment at the time of the outbreak, and was killed, but his assailants paid dearly for his death. There were two native corporals who did not join the rebels, and they also were slain.

When the Cantonment had been cleared of the British officers, the mutineers proceeded to the large district jail, and released the prisoners. The court-house was then burned. Then followed the burning of bungalows in the Cantonment. After this the mutineers went to the city

PRINCIPAL ENTRANCE TO JHANSI.

and made it their first object to lay hold upon all natives who had been in the service of the British, especially those who were known to have rendered them assistance during the occurrence of recent events, but it is not known what treatment such persons received.

The sad story of the fate of those who had taken refuge in the city fort remains to be told. Captains Skene and Gordon had done what they could with the slender resources at their command to arrange for the defence of themselves, and their fellow-refugees. The few rifles which had been taken to the fort had been distributed, and positions had been assigned to different individuals. The ladies were told off to cast bullets and to prepare food. Piles of stones had been heaped up behind the fort gates to prevent them from being forced open. Having made such preparations as these, the little company awaited with anxiety the expected onset of the rebels.

A feeble attack was made with only one gun on the afternoon of the 6th. As the rebels approached the fort, they were received with a well-directed fire, which caused them to fall back in confusion. Their firing, which was without effect, was kept up until nightfall.

The mutineers then withdrew, leaving a strong guard of the Rani's followers to prevent the escape of any one from the fort during the night. It is said that the beleaguered party meditated a flight that night, but daylight approaching before they had completed their plan, the attempt was abandoned. On the following night, however, one of the party (a Mr. Crawford) succeeded in making good his escape.

On the evening of the 6th a meeting was held of the mutineer leaders and delegates from the Rani to settle the question of the future Government, and to decide as to what should be done with the British officers and other Europeans in the fort. Some were in favor of letting them all go away in safety, but this suggestion was opposed and overruled by a Mahomedan, named Bakhshish Ali, the ex-superintendent of the jail, and their destruction was decided on. The question of the Government was not settled at this time, as the Rani's representatives and the mutineers could not come to terms. The mutineer party had bethought themselves of a clever piece of diplomacy. Having an eye to extensive personal profit by the overthrow of the British administration, they thought to further their design by creating competition among possible rivals for the rulership, hoping by this means to extort from the Rani a good price for restoring her to authority. At Unao, a town five miles from Jhansi, resided an illegitimate relation of the late Raja, who had on a previous occasion put forward a claim to the headship of the Principality. This man, Sadasheo Rao by name, was invited by the mutineers to come to Jhansi, and he came with the intention of bidding for the throne, but he did not arrive until the 8th, when he set up his camp in the Cantonment, close to the star fort. Meanwhile a proclamation was issued in the following terms:—"The people are God's; the country is the Padshah's (the King's, whoever he may be); and the two religions (the Hindu and the Mohamedan) govern." It is stated that this proclamation was not made until the evening of that day of sad and awful memories in the annals of Jhansi, the 8th of June.

It was evident to Captains Skene and Gordon that they and their comrades could not long hold out against the rebels, as guns, ammunition, provisions and water, except in very limited quantities, were all wanting. On the morning of the 7th, therefore, they decided upon sending three of their number under a safe-conduct (if procurable) to treat with the Rani, hoping that they might be allowed to retire to some place of safety in British territory. Accordingly it was arranged that Messrs. A. Scott, C. Purcell and J. Purcell should proceed to the palace. As no arrangement could be made for a safe escort, they went forth risking their lives. They had not gone far before they were seized by the rebels and taken to the palace gate. When the Rani was apprised of their presence at her door, her reply to the announcement was, "I have no concern with the English swine"; but she ordered the prisoners to be taken to the head-quarters of the Irregular Cavalry. This command was equivalent to the issuing of the death-warrant of these men. One account states that they were put to death at the cavalry head-quarters, another mentions that they were killed just beyond the wall of the city. Subsequently Mr. T. Andrews, who had left the fort, was seized and killed by the Rani's own servants at the palace door. During the day Captains Skene and Gordon sent a number of communications to the Rani, and replies were received from her, but the contents of the correspondence are not known. About two o'clock in the afternoon another attack was made on the fort, and the assault was continued until nightfall. Some of the rebels were killed in the attack, but none of the besieged were hurt.

Soon after daybreak on the 8th of June, cannons supplied by the Rani, and other small field-pieces brought from the Cantonment, having been placed in position, the mutineers opened a brisk fire against the walls of the fort. Whether from any defect in the guns, or want of skill in using them, this cannonading proved utterly ineffective. Not a single stone in the walls was, according to the statement of a native spectator, displaced by the fire.

While this assault was proceeding, a deed of treachery within the fort was discovered. Two natives, who had been servants of the British Government in the survey department, were found to be acting in concert with the rebels outside, having been caught in an attempt to open the door of a secret passage communicating with the town. Lieut. Powis, who discovered this, shot one of the culprits, but he was himself mortally wounded by the other, who in his turn was killed by Lieut. Burgess, and the two traitors were laid side by side in a trench and buried. That day some Eurasians stole out of the fort, hoping to be able to save their lives, but they were seized and put to death.

An escalade was finally attempted by the besiegers, but it failed, as all who were engaged in it were shot down by the garrison. The attack, however, was continued, and during the afternoon the mutineers with guns and elephants were able to force open the outer gates, and soon after this to establish themselves in the lower portions of the fort. The crisis seemed to be approaching. With the heroism of a last hope the holders of the fort exerted themselves in its defence, Skene and Gordon especially sending many a message of death to the assailants. At length Capt. Gordon, who was looking through a window over the fort gate, and whose familiar face was recognized, was aimed at and shot. Upon the occurrence of this event a heavy cloud of despondency gathered over the remainder of the defenders, for Gordon had been the life and soul of the garrison, and it began to be felt by them that as they could not hold out much longer it would be better to surrender. In a short time, therefore, Skene intimated to the enemy that the garrison was ready to make terms of peace. Upon this the leaders of the insurgents drawing near to the gate, and hearing what Skene had to propose, swore with the most solemn and sacred oaths, through the medium of Saleh Mahomed, a native doctor, that all the British and Anglo-Indians in the fort would be allowed to depart in safety, if they would give themselves up. Confidence more or less was placed in these assurances, the gates were thrown open, and the helpless band walked out of the fort only to be apprehended by the rebels, who immediately bound the men of the party, lest any of them should escape. Presently some sepoys of the cavalry came riding up, and announced that it was the order of their officer that all the captives should be put to death. The prisoners were then led forth without the city wall to the Jokhan Bagh in the direction of the star fort to be massacred. The leader in this foul proceeding was the infamous ex-superintendent of the jail, who first with his own sword cut down Capt. Skene. Dr. McEgan seems to have been the next victim. His wife tried to save him by throwing her arms around him, but she was beaten and pushed aside. Dr. McEgan was then cut down, and Mrs. McEgan, who cast herself upon her husband's prostrate body was also killed. It is said that a Miss Brown fell on her knees before a sepoy, and begged for her life, but she was immediately cut down. No particulars concerning the deaths of the others are recorded, but all perished together, the whole number of the unhappy victims of the mutiny in Jhansi, including those who were killed in the Cantonment, being 66. A Eurasian woman, Mrs. Mutlow, escaped being massacred, by having at the time of the outbreak concealed herself in the town, disguised as a native. Some of the bodies of the slain were allowed to remain unburied for several days. When they were buried, the remains of the men were thrown into one gravel pit, and those of the women into another. Then all were lightly covered.

On the 9th of June, after the Rani and Sadasheo Rao had had an opportunity of bidding against each other for the headship of the territory which had been cleared of its British rulers, the matter of the new Government was settled in the Rani's favor by her paying down to the mutineers a large sum of money, and promising to pay more in the future. A new proclamation was then made as follows:—"The people are God's; the country is the Padsha's (by which was probably meant the Paramount Power in India); and the Raj (Rule) is Rani Lakshmi Bai's."

The disappointed aspirant to the chieftainship of Jhansi was not inclined to return quietly to his village home. There is in the district, at the distance of 30 miles from Jhansi, a strong Bundela fort called Kurrara. It was the head-quarters of the Bundelas before they established their capital at Orcha. To this fort Sadasheo Rao betook himself with such a following as he could command, which is said to have numbered 300 men. He turned out the British native officials who were still there, appointed his own officers of state, and issued a proclamation to this effect:—"Maharaja Sadasheo Rao Narayan has seated himself on the throne of Jhansi, at Kurrara." Shortly afterwards, however, the Rani sent some troops against him, and he fled into the territory of Scindia. But he was subsequently inveigled by the Rani into her power, and after the retaking of Jhansi by the British in 1858 he was transported for life.

The Rani at once set to work most vigorously to establish her authority in her old capital. She levied troops, strengthened the fortifications of Jhansi and Kurrara, and started a mint for the coining of her own currency. She governed ostensibly on behalf of her adopted son, and at the same time endeavored to gain the favor of the British Government by writing to several high officials, lamenting the massacre which had taken place in Jhansi, with which she disavowed having had any connection whatever. She asserted that she was only holding the Jhansi district until the British could make arrangements for reoccupying it. The Rani remained in power until April 1858, when by the advent of a British army and its operations against the doomed city the whole situation was again changed.

VII.

THE RE-TAKING OF JHANSI BY MAJOR-GENERAL SIR HUGH ROSE, AND THE FLIGHT OF THE RANI.

In the summer of 1857 the British were so fully occupied in quelling the outbreaks of mutiny at Delhi, Cawnpore, Lucknow and other places in North India, that they were unable to undertake any military operations in Central India before the spring of the following year.

The officer who was chosen to command a column of Bombay troops, which, starting from the large cantonment of Mhow, marched to Jhansi, Kalpi and Gwalior, was Major-General Sir Hugh Rose, who was afterwards Commander-in-Chief of the Army in India, and entitled Lord Strathnairn. He was the most conspicuous figure in the Central India Campaign, the events of which form one of the most thrilling chapters in the history of the Sepoy War. During a military and diplomatic career, which had already extended over thirty-seven years, he had been employed in Ireland and in Syria, and had taken part in the engagements at the Alma, at Inkermann and before Sevastopol. Not the least of the services which he had rendered to his country were those which he performed as a diplomatist at Beyrout and at Constantinople. The fearlessness of responsibility, and the promptness of action, which ever characterized him were splendidly illustrated, when at an important crisis of strategic manœuvering on the part of the representatives of Russia and England, he was the alert and daring instrument of checkmating Prince Menschikoff by ordering the British fleet at Malta to proceed at once to Besika Bay.

When General Rose was appointed to conduct in conjunction with General Whitlock the Central India Campaign, he was altogether new to India; and his being entrusted with a large share of so important an undertaking as the subjugating of the numerous rebel hordes, which infested the country between the Nerbudda and Jumna rivers, was regarded by some who were aware of the magnitude of the task to be performed, as a very grave experiment, but all doubt as to his fitness for the position assigned to him was dispelled as his movements were observed. From the first he appeared to have "an instinctive perception of the conditions of success in Indian warfare," and his brilliant achievements abundantly justified the wisdom of those who selected him for a service of so great responsibility. Further justification of the wisdom of the selection of Sir Hugh Rose for this service in India was furnished, when through the failure of General Whitlock to join him, he proved himself capable of conducting virtually the entire campaign alone, and of accomplishing with a single column of troops the task which two columns were set to do. Had an officer less competent than General Rose been appointed to the command of the Bombay column, it is not improbable that a humiliating and most disastrous failure would have been the result, and that historians of the campaign would have had to record, instead of a chapter of marvellous successes, the defeat of a British army by a Mahratta heroine, who suddenly, by the force of circumstances, developed into one of the bravest of warriors. "The best and bravest military leader of the rebels," are the words with which Sir Hugh Rose himself expressed his esteem for the young Rani of Jhansi as a soldier. Col. Malleson in his history speaks of her as "a woman who possessed all the instincts, all the courage, all the resolution of a warrior of the type so well known in consular Rome."

After various successful engagements with rebel forces on his way to Jhansi, in one of which his horse was shot under him, he arrived with his second brigade on the 20th of March within fourteen miles of that place, and after a short rest sent forward a part of his force to reconnoitre and invest the city. As the British troops approached nearer and nearer to the theatre of the sad events of the previous summer, keener and keener became their interest in every move which was made by their Commander, and greater and greater grew the consternation of those within the doomed city who dreaded the onset of the avengers, of whose approach they had not been unwarned. As early as the 14th instant a council of war had been held by the Rani and her advisers. Some, who had been serving her in various administrative offices, urged her to make terms without engaging in a conflict. Others, among them the sepoys who had rallied to her support, pressed her to fight. The former insisted that it would not only be useless, but the height of madness, for them to attempt to oppose the invincible British. The latter, appealing to the valorous spirit which they knew the Rani to possess, said that it would be unworthy of her to yield without a struggle that which she had so resolutely acquired. This appeal was successful, although there is good reason for believing that the Rani, if she had not been overborne by the influence of the sepoys, rather than have a single shot fired, would have preferred to sue for mercy. Conversations which the writer has had with old men in the city have elicited the remark, which seems to express the general belief, that "the Bai (the Lady) did not wish to fight against the British."

The garrison of the Rani numbered eleven thousand five hundred men, including fifteen hundred sepoys who had been trained in the British army. The column of troops with General Rose included two brigades, comprising two regiments of European infantry, one regiment of European cavalry, four regiments of native infantry, four regiments of native cavalry, bodies of artillery, sappers and miners, and a siege train. Numerically the forces of the Rani and those of the British General were about equal.

General Rose at the head of the second brigade set out from his camp at two o'clock on the morning of the 21st of March, and arrived before Jhansi at nine o'clock. Halting his troops at the distance of a mile and a half from the fort, he and his staff, with an escort, very soon proceeded to reconnoitre the position of the enemy. How carefully the whole situation was studied may be inferred from the fact that the General did not return to his camp until six o'clock that evening.

Stretching between the open ground on which he had halted and the wall of the city were the charred ruins of the bungalows in which had dwelt the British officers who ten months before had been slain.

Of the fort and city of Jhansi after they had fallen into his hands, the following description, taken almost textually from his despatch of April 30th, was given by Sir Hugh Rose:—The great strength of the fort of

Jhansi, natural as well as artificial, and its extent, entitle it to a place among fortresses. It stands on an elevated rock, rising out of a plain, and commands the city and surrounding country. It is built of excellent and most massive masonry. The fort is difficult to breach, because composed of granite; its walls vary in thickness from sixteen to twenty feet. It has extensive and elaborate outworks of the same solid construction, with front and flanking embrasures for artillery-fire, and loop-holes, of which there were in some places five tiers, for musketry. Guns placed on the high towers of the fort commanded the country all around. On one tower, called the "white turret," recently raised in height, waved in proud defiance the standard of the high-spirited Rani. The fortress is surrounded on all sides by the city, the west and part of the south face excepted. The steepness of the rock protects the west; the fortified city wall springs from the centre of its south face, runs south-east, and ends in a high mound or mamelon, which protects by a flanking fire its south face. The mound was fortified by a strong circular bastion for five guns, round part of which was drawn a ditch, twelve feet deep and fifteen feet broad, of solid masonry. The city is surrounded by a fortified massive wall from six to twelve feet thick, and varying in height from eighteen to thirty feet, with numerous flanking bastions armed as batteries, with ordnance, and loop-holes, and with a banquette for infantry.

One result of the General's long reconnaissance on the 21st of March was the decision to take the city before assaulting the fort. To besiege the fort before taking the city would, he thought, involve double labor and double danger. The wisdom of the course which he had decided upon was shown, when after the taking of the city, the fort was abandoned by its defenders. The

General's reconnaissance did not end until he had fully decided upon his plan of attack. He had determined to make his assault upon the city from two directions, from the east and from the south. On a rocky knoll on the eastern side of the city, and about three hundred yards from the city wall, four batteries were placed for the purpose of bombarding the city. While these batteries were being placed in position, the General effected with the cavalry of the first brigade, which joined him on the night of the 21st, a more complete investment of the city than had previously been made, which procedure served to inform the insurgents that it was the intention of the British Commander, not only to take the city and the fort, but to capture, if possible, the entire garrison. The four batteries were ready for action on the morning of the 24th, and on the morning of the 25th the bombardment of the city was commenced.

The chief point to be assaulted, however, was the fortified mound, which formed a part of the city wall toward the south. Of this we have already given General Rose's own description. As the wall could be breached more easily at that place than at any other, the rebels had endeavored to strengthen that point to the utmost. It was, as far as the fortifications on the city wall were concerned, their stronghold. For this reason General Rose had determined to take it, and through a breach to be made there to effect an entrance into the city. This mound was called by the besiegers the Mamelon. About four hundred yards distant from it was a rocky eminence from which the assault upon it was made, the guns placed there being two 18-pounders. When on the 25th of March the remainder of the first brigade arrived, these troops were posted to the south of the city. The forces belonging to the second brigade on the eastern side of the city, and those of the first brigade on the south, were designated respectively the "Right Attack" and the "Left Attack."

When all preparations had been completed, the siege was prosecuted in earnest. While the gunners unceasingly bombarded the city from the east, and the Mamelon from the south, the infantry kept up a galling fire against the rebels who lined the walls. On account of the terrific heat at that season, the ordeal to which the European soldiers were subjected was most severe, but during the long day they ceased not from their exhausting toil. By keeping wet towels bound round their heads they were able in some measure to mitigate the effect of the burning sun and the hot wind, and they were stimulated to exertion by seeing their General sharing their hardship as he went from point to point for the purpose of cheering his men.

In defending the city the rebels showed great courage and determination. It is said that the Rani constantly visited the defences, and that her presence and words had a great effect in animating the garrison. Women were seen actively engaged in distributing ammunition and even in working the batteries, and children as well as women assisted in repairing damages occasioned by the siege, and in carrying food and water to the men and women on the wall. Frequent fires occurred in the city, as houses were ignited by the bursting of shells, and the consternation of the beleaguered people rapidly increased as they saw more and more of the havoc wrought by the besiegers on every side, and as lamentations for the dead and wounded were multiplied.

On account of the great strength of the Mamelon, the progress made in besieging it was slow, but on the 29th of March the parapets of its

THE BREACHED MAMELON.

bastion were levelled, and its guns were silenced. On the two following days the cannonading by both sides was kept up with increased energy and excitement. It is said that the fire of the rebels was so incessant that the parapet of the city wall and the ramparts of the fortress all along often presented the appearance of a sheet of flame. On the 30th a breach was effected, but it was promptly and with great bravery stockaded. The besiegers then opened a fire of red hot shot, by which much of the stockade was readily destroyed. As, however, the breach was not yet practicable, the bombardment was still being most vigorously prosecuted, and the rebels were continuing the defence with unabated courage, when on the evening of the 31st the strenuous efforts alike of the British forces and of the rebels were suddenly but only momentarily suspended. The British heard, and the rebels saw, from the fortress, that an army was approaching from the south. Tantia Topi was coming with a great force to the relief of the Rani. His coming was not unanticipated by the Rani and her people, for she had written to him beseeching him to come to her help, and the hope of being rescued by him from a perilous position had served to inspire her and her troops with fresh fortitude from day to day. Nor was the coming of Tantia a surprise to Sir Hugh Rose. He knew that this famous rebel leader had been besieging the town and fort of Charkhari, eighty miles east of Jhansi, and he had reason to believe that his next move would be to come to the Rani's aid. He was therefore expecting him to appear, and in accordance with this expectation he had on the night of the 30th ordered out a large force from both brigades and led it himself to the bank of the Betwa river, eight miles distant. As nothing was seen or heard of the enemy, the force returned. On the next evening, however, the General's expectation was realized, and suddenly great commotion occurred in the camps of the two brigades. On this, as on all other occasions, General Rose remained calm in the midst of the excitement which prevailed among his troops, and quietly attended to the arrangement of his plans. He had wisely determined that the siege should not be intermitted, but that it should be continued with unabated vigor. He could not, however, safely withdraw, from both brigades more than fifteen hundred men of all arms, and of these only five hundred were Europeans, but he determined to go forth himself with only these, to encounter an army of rebels numbering no less than twenty-two thousand. This great rebel force, moreover, was being led by a General who only four months before at Cawnpore had defeated Major-General Windham, the hero of the Redan, and flushed with the victory, and enriched by the abundant spoils, which it had just gained at Charkhari, it was confident of success at Jhansi. The situation of the British force at this juncture was indeed critical. If ever a cool brain and judicious as well as brave generalship were needed in a military commander in a great emergency, it was at this time when General Rose was obliged to confront with a force numerically so inferior the swarming multitude of rebels led by Tantia, and containing five or six regiments of sepoys which had been trained by British officers. It was no light thing for General Rose to leave in his rear so large a body of exultant rebels, who, spurred to the utmost by "a woman of genius and masculine resolution," might by some sudden onset gain an advantage over the troops which remained to continue the siege; but he had made as good a disposition of his forces as was possible, and with as clear a head and as brave a heart as British soldier ever possessed, he resolved to dare and do his best.

As Colonel Malleson well remarks, "the position of Sir Hugh Rose was full of peril. It required in a special degree great daring, a resolute will, the power to take responsibility. A single false step, a solitary error in judgment, might have been fatal. But Sir Hugh Rose was equal to the occasion."

General Rose resolved not to remain on the defensive, but to attack the enemy early the next morning. The movements of the British General were observed with the greatest interest by the rebels in the fort and especially by the Rani, for all felt sure that the small British force was going forth to certain destruction. It is said that during the whole of the preceding night they had been shouting with frantic delight at the prospect of what they would witness in the morning.

Colonel Malleson in his history has given a detailed and graphic account of the engagement with Tantia's troops and the utter overthrow of his army; he has also given full and interesting particulars of the final struggle with the Jhansi rebels, which immediately ensued. The following is taken almost verbatim from his carefully compiled narratives:—Sir Hugh had drawn his force from both brigades, the detachments from the first being led by Brigadier C. S. Stuart, that from the second by himself in person. The men had slept in their clothes in order to be ready for immediate action. This precaution had wisely been taken. At four o'clock on the morning of the 1st of April Tantia's troops advanced towards the British encampment. Half an hour later the falling back of the pickets warned the British General of the near approach of the enemy. In a few minutes the British guns opened fire, and almost immediately those of the opposing force answered. The fire of the few guns of the British was powerless to check the onward march of an army whose line overlapped that of the British on both flanks. Tantia's force had but to move straight on to reach with its extended wings the British troops which were besieging the fortress, which troops if thus reached would be placed between two enfilading fires. Sir Hugh comprehended the situation in an instant, and took measures to meet it. Massing his horse artillery on his left, and attaching to it a squadron of the Light Dragoons, he ordered them to attack the enemy's right, whilst he himself, on the other flank should direct another squadron against their left. The plan succeeded admirably. The rebels were so surprised and intimidated by this double attack, that their centre, which up to that time had been advancing steadily, first halted, and then, as the men composing it discerned a movement on the part of the British infantry, broke up into disordered masses. This movement of the British infantry was in obedience to an order of General Rose to advance as soon as the cavalry attack should be well pronounced. When they sprang to their feet, advanced a few yards, discharged a volley into the enemy's ranks and then rushed upon them with fixed bayonets, the effect was magical. The first line of Tantia's troops at once broke, and fled in complete disorder towards the second line, abandoning several guns.

The second line, commanded by Tantia in person, was occupying a position upon rising ground, its front covered by jungle, about two miles in rear of the first line. Tantia beheld in dismay the latter rushing helter skelter towards him, followed by the three arms of the British in hot pursuit; but he had scarcely realized the fact, when another vision on his right flank appeared, to add to his anguish. Whilst Sir Hugh Rose had been engaged in the manner described, Brigadier Stuart with his force had moved around into the plain on the right of the enemy, in order to check a large body of them, who were taking advantage of the battle raging in front of the line to move off towards the city. Stuart attacked them, and defeating them drove them back, hotly following them. So close indeed was the pursuit, that this detachment of Tantia's troops having no time to re-form, fled in confusion, leaving gun after gun in the hands of the victors, and leaving also numbers of their dead or dying on the field.

This had the effect of forcing upon Tantia a sudden decision. The day he saw was lost ; but there was yet time, he hoped, to save his second line and his remaining guns. He at once set fire to the dry jungle which covered the ground between him and the British, and then under the cover of the smoke and flames commenced a retreat towards the Betwa, hoping to be able to place that river between himself and his pursuers. His infantry and horsemen led the retreat, and his artillery covered it. Right gallantly and skilfully they did it, and he succeeded in crossing the river with his reserve and guns and some of the fugitives from the first line, but he was not the safer for the passage. The British horse artillery and cavalry had dashed at a gallop through the burning jungle, and they were resolved not to cease from the pursuit till they had captured every gun that had opened against them. They carried out their intention to the letter. Every gun was taken. Twenty-eight field-pieces were brought back with them when they rejoined their comrades that evening. Fifteen hundred rebels had been killed or wounded, and the remainder, with Tantia at their head, fled towards Kalpi.

Whilst the battle with Tantia's army had been raging, the besieged had redoubled their fire. Mounting the bastions and the wall, they had shouted and yelled and poured forth volleys of musketry, apparently threatening a sortie. The batteries of the besiegers were never plied with more vigour or with greater effect. The sight from the wall, however, did not long continue to inspire. Suddenly the yells and the shouts ceased, for the garrison had recognized the fact that the day of their deliverance had not arrived, as they had confidently expected.

The victorious troops, returning from the pursuit of Tantia's army with their *morale* greatly strengthened, resumed at once their former positions at the siege. The British General, having determined to take advantage of the discouragement which he knew the defeat of Tantia could not have failed to produce in the minds of the besieged, ordered that heavy firing should be kept up all that night; and it was continued during all the next day. On the 2nd of April the breach in the city wall having been rendered practicable, Sir Hugh resolved to storm the place the next morning, and made his preparations accordingly.

His plan was to make a false attack on the west wall with a detachment under Major Gall of the 14th Light Dragoons, and as soon as the sound of his guns should be heard, the main storming party was to debouch from cover and enter the breach, whilst on the right of the breach an attempt should be made to escalade the wall. Such was the programme to be followed by the "Left Attack," which was composed of the Royal Engineers, the 86th Foot, and the 25th Bombay Native infantry. Its left column, commanded by Lt.-Col. Lowth, was to storm the breach; its right column, led by Major Stuart, was to escalade the wall to the right of the breach.

The reserve was commanded by Brigadier Stuart. The "Right Attack," on the eastern side of the city, was to escalade the eastern wall. Of these troops, comprising the Madras and Bombay Sappers, the 3rd Bombay Europeans, and the Infantry of the Hyderabad Contingent, the right column was commanded by Lt.-Col. Liddell, the left by Capt. Robinson, and the reserve by Brigadier Steuart of the 14th Light Dragoons.

At 3 A. M. on the 3rd of April the storming parties marched to the positions which had been assigned to them and awaited the signal to be given by Major Gall's party. No sooner was it heard than the stormers dashed to the front. On the left Capt. Darby led the troops of Col. Lowth's column in the most gallant manner up the slope towards the Mamelon. On approaching near the wall the progress of the stormers was impeded by a deep trench, the existence of which was previously unknown to the besiegers, because it was entirely hidden from their view. To leap into this trench, plant the ladders, and ascend on the side towards the wall, was however but the work of a few moments. A young soldier, named Dartnell, was the first to gain the breach ; but the ladder by which he ascended the wall having been broken by the impetuosity of those who were following him, he was momentarily left alone to be hacked at by the rebels. He was severely wounded, and only saved his life by receiving in his arm the sabre cuts which were aimed at his head. With such determination did the stormers push forward and pour through the breach that the main body of the rebels who had been defending the Mamelon speedily took to flight. The few brave defenders who stood their ground were killed, and thus that part of the wall which had borne the brunt of the siege was entirely cleared. Down the incline towards the street, leading from the principal gate of the city to the palace, rushed the British troops.

Simultaneously with the attack just described, Major Stuart, though steadily opposed by the enemy, had effected another entrance into the town by escalading the wall at a short distance to the right of the Mamelon. Thus with eminent success had the stormers of the "Left Attack" gone forward.

As soon as an entrance into the city had been effected on the south side, Col. Lowth despatched a part of his force to aid the stormers of the "Right Attack," who had not yet won any success. This detachment, attacking in flank and rear the rebels who were defending the eastern wall, forced them to retire, thus clearing the way for the entrance of the British troops on the eastern side of the city.

The troops of the "Right Attack" had suffered severely in their fruitless attempt to scale the eastern wall. On hearing the signal given by Major Gall's men, they had marched silently from their cover in three bodies. No sooner however had they turned into the road leading to the Saugor gate, which was the object of their assault, than the enemy's bugles sounded an alarm, and at once a very heavy fire was opened upon them. "For a time," says one who was there, "it appeared like a sheet of fire, out of which burst a storm of bullets, round-shot and rockets, destined for our annihilation." Through this fire the stormers had to march upwards of two hundred yards, but they pushed on steadily and planted their ladders in three places against the wall. For the moment, however, it was impossible for them to ascend. Amid a chaos of sounds of volleys of musketry, and of the roaring of cannon, and of the hissing and bursting of rockets and infernal machines, and while huge stones,

A BIT OF THE EASTERN WALL.

blocks of wood, and even trees were being hurled upon them, the assailants were obliged to pause for a little and shelter themselves as best they could. The Sappers, however, kept firm hold of their ladders, and in spite of the prodigious efforts of the enemy maintained them in their positions against the wall. How long this check continued no one could tell, for minutes then seemed to be hours. When the pause occurred, Major Boileau, of the Madras Engineers, went back to report the state of affairs to the Brigadier, and he quickly brought up a reinforcement of one hundred men of the 3rd Europeans. Then the stormers, led by their engineer officers, rushed to the ladders. Unfortunately some of the ladders were found to be too short, while others from weakness broke down under the weight of the men. Lieut. Dick, of the Engineers, was the first to gain by means of one of the ladders the summit of the wall. While fighting against enormous odds he called out to the men to follow him. Lieut. Meiklejohn mounted by another ladder, and then boldly jumped down amongst the rebels below. The men pressed on from behind, but before they could, in any number, join their officers, Dick had fallen from the wall dying, having received numerous wounds, both from shot and bayonet; Meiklejohn had been cut to pieces; and Fox, of the Madras Sappers, who had also reached the top of the wall, had been shot in the neck. But the stormers pushed on, ascending by eight or more ladders, and at length gained a footing on the wall, where they and their antagonists contested the position most fiercely, and death was dealt out to many on both sides.

It was at this crisis that the detachment from the "Left Attack" came to the aid of their comrades on the eastern wall, and relieved them by taking their assailants in flank and rear, thus compelling them to withdraw from the defence on that side of the city. Being thus succored, the stormers of the "Right Attack" were able to join those of the "Left," and take part in clearing the road to the palace, situated about three hundred yards from the fort.

Throughout the entire length of this thoroughfare the British troops were obliged to fight their way, and here the struggle with the rebels was terrible in the extreme, for it was for the most part a house-to-house and hand-to-hand encounter with an infuriated mob. As the conflict raged, the street was strewed with the bodies of the dead and dying; and the flames of burning houses, intensifying the heat of an April sun, made the temperature in the narrow road wellnigh unendurable. The road as it approached the palace ran near the fort, and on the side towards the fort there were no buildings to shield them. Here consequently for a considerable distance the British troops were exposed to a heavy musketry fire from the crowds of rebels on the fortress wall which towered above them, and very many were either killed or wounded, among whom were quite a number of officers. Here were found General Rose and his staff, leading the troops on to the palace. "There was," says an eye-witness, "one individual whose attention to the wounded and dying must have attracted every one's notice. He was always present by day and by night, regardless of danger: he seemed animated but by one desire, which was to do good and afford consolation to the dying, whether Catholic or Protestant. This was the Rev. Mr. Strickland."

At the palace occurred the most sanguinary conflict of this awful day. The residence of the Rani had been specially prepared for resistance in the last resort. The

THE RANI'S PALACE.

courtyard was the scene of the first bloody encounter. Access to each apartment in turn was most stubbornly opposed, and to dislodge the rebels the bayonet was freely used. At length the struggle seemed to be at an end, but later on it was discovered that fifty men of the Rani's bodyguard still held the stables attached to the palace. These, to the last man, stood their ground, fighting to the death. A trophy most highly valued by those who captured it was obtained during the contest with these men. It was the silken Union Jack which Lord William Bentinck, when Governor-General of India, presented to the first Raja of Jhansi in recognition of his loyalty to the British.

The struggle at the palace had but just terminated when General Rose, who had been present throughout with the "Left Attack," received information that a body of rebels, numbering about four hundred, after having tried in vain to force the pickets of one of the British cavalry camps outside the city, had taken up a position on a rocky height to the west of the fortress, and that the cavalry had surrounded them there. He therefore sent Major Gall with a detachment of the Bombay Native Infantry to attack them, and all were killed but about twenty, who retreated to the summit of the crag, and there placing themselves upon their powder flasks blew themselves up. This lofty mass of rock is now called "Retribution Hill." The British lost an officer and several men in the attack upon this hill. Another body of about fifteen hundred rebels, having collected in one of the suburbs of the city, had resolved to defend themselves to the last, but when attacked they failed to stand their ground. Three hundred of these were either killed or wounded, and the remainder made good their escape. All that night and throughout the following day desultory fighting continued, and many of the enemy were killed, while others saved themselves by taking shelter under the guns of the fort.

The British losses during the operations against Jhansi, including the action with Tantia Topi, amounted to three hundred and forty-three killed and wounded, of whom thirty-six were officers. The enemy's loss was computed at five thousand.

"The mode by which Jhansi was captured," writes Col. Malleson, "attests the merits of the noble soldier who planned and carried out the attack. Never was there a more complete combination of daring and skill, of foresight and resolution. The result was worthy of the plan and of the genius which formed the plan."

Assistant Surgeon Sylvester, in recording his recollections of the taking of Jhansi, wrote as follows concerning the conduct of Sir Hugh Rose's troops:—"During the whole siege the greatest forbearance was shown to all who would peaceably surrender." He further said that the British soldiers manifested a degree of forbearance and Christian kindness towards women and children and aged men that was a great credit to them. They even shared their meals with some of the people found destitute in the city.

When the fighting had ceased, an eager search for treasure and curiosities ensued. In this officers and men alike participated, all being anxious to obtain some interesting memento of the siege and capture of Jhansi. Of what they did, and of what they found, Sylvester gives the following account:—"They dived into every house and searched its dark corners; they pulled down walls, or parts of walls, which appeared to be of recent construction, all out of curiosity, and not from a desire to loot of course, because this was for-

RETRIBUTION HILL.

bidden under pain of the strictest punishment. One class of articles, however, seemed to be looked upon as fair loot by even the most scrupulous: these were the gods found in the temples. They were collected in great numbers, and were strangely sought after by every officer and common soldier. There were Gunputies and Vishnoos innumerable and of every metal. Some were really pretty ornaments, silver with gold bangles on their grotesque limbs, and small enough to be worn on the watch-chain; others were of brass and stone of rare workmanship. So general had the rebellion been in the city that even the fakeers and gosains had left their holy places and armed against us. The chief interest centred in the palace of the Rani. Here were pet animals of various kinds. Everything was in the greatest confusion and disorder, and the open court was strewn with clothes, firearms, horse and elephant gear, cooking utensils, grass, grain, etc. The second storey had a very handsome appearance, in fact was somewhat gorgeous. The chief apartments ran the whole length of the palace front, the suite consisting of a large durbar room, two sleeping apartments, an inner *sans-souci*-looking sort of chamber, the ceiling of which was of plate-glass mirrors, and the walls of ornamental and gilded panels, decorated with mirrors and paintings. On the floor was spread a cushion of cotton, covered with crimson velvet, and one's feet sank in it as in snow. Here one pictured the Rani taking her siesta, or listening to her favorite minstrel and the twang of his guitar. The large room was beautifully painted, glazed and ornamented, and was carpeted with rugs of Persian manufacture. There were four large windows on the front side, and large chandeliers of purple-colored glass were suspended from the ceiling. The room was furnished with chairs and ottomans, tables and couches, pictures and ornaments in abundance, many of costly metal. The sleeping rooms were fitted up by one who was no stranger to luxury. In the ornamentation scarlet and gold were the prevailing colors. The bedsteads were of silver, and the coverlets were of scarlet satin and silk and gold. Women's dresses, and some very full skirts with gilt trimmings, doubtless belonging to nautch girls, were lying about. Every thing indicated the hasty and unexpected flight of the Rani. She had taken refuge in the fort probably as soon as the noise of the assault had been heard by her on the morning of the 3rd. It looked somewhat strange to see groups of men in red coats prowling about in the deserted palace, with powder-besmeared faces, and their bayonets stained with blood. Along the passages and in the verandahs were numberless brass and copper vessels, some of them of huge proportions. These were valuable, and must have constituted a considerable item in the prize account. There were some horribly dismal rooms, bringing the Italian dungeons forcibly to mind. These appeared to be store-rooms for an indescribable variety of articles. In the smaller upper rooms the valuables were found, consisting of shawls, scarfs, turbans, gold ornaments, jewels and silver vessels, together with bags of rupees and gold mohurs. But the spoil was not all found in one place or at one time. Chests of treasure were constantly being discovered by the help of the divining rods of the prize agents. Some English plate, which had belonged to some of the victims of the massacre, was recovered. Guards were placed over the treasure, and some members of the General's staff took up their abode in the palace. The town was held by the infantry and guns. The enemy held the fortress, on which their flag continued to fly. They kept up a desultory fire from their guns, and shot at all they saw from the loop-holes. It was thought they would hold out for some time."

General Rose, meanwhile, was engaged in planning for an assault upon the fortress. But whatever plan he may have resolved upon, he was spared the task of carrying it into execution; for on the night of the 4th of April the stronghold was evacuated, and the Rani and many who fled with her succeeded in making good their escape beyond the British lines. Not until daybreak was it known that the rebels had fled. One of the British pickets, seeing the fort-gate open, made known the fact to his comrades, whereupon they cautiously approached the entrance; then, not being fired upon, they, accompanied by some officers, entered and found the place entirely deserted. The Rani's red flag was still flying over the citadel, but no time was lost in removing it, and hoisting in its place the Union Jack.

It was marvellous that the Rani and any of her followers could succeed in evading detection by the British pickets. How extraordinary the achievement was, will be better understood when it is explained that the fort-gate was on the side towards the palace, and inside the city wall; and that a considerable circuit had to be traversed by the fugitives before they reached the wall-gate—the Ganpat Khirki—through which they made their exit. And having got outside the city wall, they had still to face the cordon of General Rose's videttes, which encircled the entire city and its suburbs. It is impossible under the circumstances to repress the question, How could all that multitude which issued from the fortress make their way to the outside of the city without being observed by the British pickets inside the city wall? What were the pickets doing, that such a thing could take place? It is not so difficult to understand how a considerable number of the fugitives could manage to elude the videttes outside the city. They must have separated into small parties, and sought simultaneously to break through the cordon at various points, and the videttes while able to turn many back would be powerless to prevent all from escaping. Probably only a minority of those who made good their escape from the fort and the city were able to get through the British lines outside. Many who attempted to break the cordon were halted, some while stubbornly essaying to overcome Major Gall's pickets being turned back no less than three times. Seeing how successfully so many had escaped, and among them the Rani herself, how great must have been the chagrin of the city's captors, when the chief prize, which they had hoped to capture, had so easily and needlessly slipped through their hands! Another remarkable circumstance about the escape of the Rani and so many of her followers was that they were provided with horses, without which their flight could not have been successful. Were their horses with them in the fort?* And if so, how much more remarkable it was that they with their horses could escape from the city unobserved!

It is said that the Rani rode straight to Kalpi, a distance of ninety-five miles, and that she could not have stopped long by the way; for when General Rose heard of her exit, he immediately sent some of his cavalrymen in pursuit, but the chase was in vain. "The Rani, though seen in full flight, mounted on a grey horse, and attended only by a few followers, could not be overtaken." Lieut. Dowker, it is said, came up so near to

* Since this was written the writer has been informed that there were about twenty horses in the fort.

THE MEMORIAL.

them, that he disturbed the Rani at her morning meal, but he had been wounded, and was so disabled that he could not continue the pursuit. Some of the fugitives, who managed to elude the British videttes, but who could not keep pace with the Rani in her flight, were overtaken and slain.

The place where the remains of the English and Eurasian residents who were massacred, were buried, if not the very spot where the Memorial, erected by the British Government, stands, must have been near that locality. When the burial-place was found, it was Sir Hugh Rose's wish that the remains should be re-interred, but this proved to be impracticable. A rough stone-wall was erected to protect the sacred spot, and over the remains the burial service was read by Chaplain Schwabe (Protestant), assisted by Chaplain Strickland (Roman Catholic), a large portion of the force which had operated against Jhansi, and the Major-General's staff, being present.

VIII.

THE RANI OF JHANSI TAKES THE FIELD AGAINST THE BRITISH, AND PERISHES AT GWALIOR.

The story of the remarkable woman who figures in the last two chapters would not be complete without the sequel which is now to be given. It is said that of the Rani's defenders in the fort at Jhansi some five hundred either accompanied her or followed her in her flight to Kalpi. Tantia Topi, after being routed by General Rose's troops, had set off in the direction of Kalpi, but as he had not marched rapidly, he did not reach that place until the evening of the Rani's arrival. The Rani expected to meet him there, for Kalpi, which had been the head-quarters of the infamous Nana, at the time when Tantia was sent by him with an army of twenty-five thousand to fight General Windham at Cawnpore, was now the head-quarters of the Nana's nephew, the Rao Sahib, under whose direction Tantia was campaigning in Bundelkhand.

When Sir Hugh Rose set out upon his Central India Campaign, his plan—a plan which at the request of the Governor-General of India had been sketched by Sir Robert Hamilton, his Agent in Central India, and which had received the endorsement of Sir Colin Campbell, the Commander-in-Chief of the Indian Army—was to be completed by the capture of Kalpi, after the stronghold of the rebels at Jhansi had been taken. Kalpi, situated on the southern bank of the Jumna river, at the distance of forty-five miles from Cawnpore, had been well chosen by the mutineer leaders as a strategic point, and as a rallying place for bands of rebels from all quarters. As the gate of Western Bundelkhand, it furnished the insurgents with an advantageous base for military operations in Central India. Here was their arsenal, which was well stocked with guns and war material of every kind.

The Rani fled to Kalpi that she might join other rebels there, and herself take the field against the British. Her first act on arriving at the rebel head-quarters was to beg the Rao Sahib "to give her an army that she might go to fight." On the morning following her arrival, the Rao held a parade of all his troops, which then consisted of a number of regiments of the Gwalior Contingent, several battalions of regular sepoys recruited to nearly their full strength (all formerly belonging to the British), the contingents of various rebel Rajas, and the remnant of the Jhansi garrison—a really formidable force. At the close of the review, the Rao addressed the troops, and then directed Tantia to take command of them, and go forth to oppose the British, who were expected soon to advance upon Kalpi.

The object of the rebel leader in sending forth his troops to meet the army of General Rose was to harass it, and if possible wear out at least the European portion of it, before it should reach its goal, for it was known to be in a very exhausted condition from fighting in the sun. And to render their opposition to the British as effective as possible, the rebel leaders agreed among themselves to make no attacks upon the British before ten o'clock in the day, in order that the "European infidels" might the more readily succumb to the heat, and consequently either die or be sent into hospital. Although Tantia Topi was placed in command of the Rao Sahib's troops, the Rani of Jhansi was no insignificant factor in the rebel army in its last encounters with the British. From the time she joined it at Kalpi, her presence and her bravery inspired it with fresh enthusiasm. Her unfailing intrepidity of spirit placed her in striking contrast with cowardly Tantia, and her astonishing power of physical endurance, coupled with other soldierly qualities, made her conspicuous as a cavalry leader. In horsemanship, in sword-practice and in the use of firearms she showed herself to be no novice. In all these arts she had been tutored from the time of her husband's death, having no doubt thought that some day they might stand her in good stead. And though previous to her joining the other rebels at Kalpi she had never taken the field against an enemy, it is possible that she may have acquired some knowledge of military tactics from observing, if not in directing, the various actions of her defenders in their warfare with the troops of the Orcha State, when the latter during the brief period which elapsed between the massacre of the English in Jhansi and the coming of Sir Hugh Rose's army to retake the place, sought to recover for their Bundela Chief the territory which Orcha had lost more than one hundred and sixty years before through the incursions of the Mahrattas.

The place where the rebels had determined to make their stand for the purpose of resisting the British army, was the town of Koonch, situated forty miles from Kalpi, and about ten miles from the main road leading to Jhansi. Here they fortified themselves, and awaited the coming of the British force.

General Rose was obliged to remain for nearly three weeks in Jhansi not only that his troops might have a little respite after the severe strain to which they had been subjected during the siege and capture of the Rani's Capital, but also that he might collect supplies and ammunition for the remainder of his campaign, and arrange for the safety of that part of Bundelkhand which he had just conquered and was about to leave in his rear.

He with his force set out for Kalpi on the 25th of April, and in six days having traversed somewhat less than half the distance to his destination, learned that the enemy was entrenched at Koonch, about fifteen miles further on, and was prepared for a stubborn resistance. As Sir Hugh's troops, having suffered greatly from the extreme heat on the six days' march, were in no condition to attack Tantia's much larger force, which after throwing up entrenchments had been resting until the British should appear, their Commander, whose judgment could be relied upon to deal an effective blow when the enemy was least prepared for it, and who also well knew when it was wise to wait in order to deprive the enemy of an advantage, decided to halt until the position which Tantia had taken up could be thoroughly reconnoitred, and his own troops were in a state to attack without serious danger of their being repulsed. This course which General Rose decided upon was the more necessary, since before making an attack, a distance of at least fourteen miles had to be travelled by his force before it would come in sight of the enemy's entrenchments. At length, on the 5th of May, the British General was ready to move forward, and before daybreak on the 6th the march was begun. The day was well advanced, and the terrific heat of the sun was making sad havoc of Sir Hugh's officers and men before the battle was over, but sagacious strategy and wise generalship won an overwhelming victory. The rebels lost more than five hundred men in killed and wounded, while the British loss, besides those who were struck down by the sun, was three officers and fifty-nine men killed and wounded. The rebels left all their guns, nine in number, on the field. The British cavalry and horse artillery entered upon the pursuit of the retreating rebels, but the pursuers were soon obliged to turn back, as their horses were so worn out that they could barely walk. Some of the fugitives were seized with heat-apoplexy, and fell dead upon the road. The Rani escaped to Kalpi, accompanied by her Jhansi horsemen. Tantia, abandoning his army before the battle was over, fled to his village home, which was about twenty miles distant. This conduct of his, coupled with his non-appearance at Kalpi, seems to indicate clearly that he considered it useless for the rebels to attempt to withstand another attack of General Rose's army, and that consequently all hope for the success of their cause was at an end.

Not so thought the Rani of Jhansi. So far from being disheartened on account of the defeat at Koonch, she was prepared to prolong the struggle with the British indefinitely, and was eager for the conflict at Kalpi. Of all the rebels who had fought at Koonch she was almost the only one who on account of their disastrous defeat had not become dispirited. It is stated concerning Tantia's beaten troops that on their way back to the Rao Sahib's head-quarters, not only did all ranks join in heaping reproach upon their cowardly commander, but they quarrelled among themselves over the disaster which had befallen them, the infantry blaming the cavalry for having deserted them at the critical moment, and the cavalry retaliating in like fashion; and that so distrustful of one another, and so discouraged and demoralised had they become, that on the day after their return, hearing that the British were advancing upon them, they dispersed, some in one direction and others in other directions, until not more than eleven sepoys could be counted in the defences at Kalpi. Even the Rani's valor was not of itself sufficient to inspire with fresh courage the disheartened followers of pusillanimous Tantia.

But for an unexpected event which occurred a few days afterwards there might have been no more fighting. This event, which was hailed with delight by the Rao Sahib and the Rani, was the arrival of the Nawab of Banda with a force of two thousand mutineer cavalry-men and some guns, besides his own followers. The troops of Tantia, scattered in the country round about, soon heard of the advent in Kalpi of the Nawab and his force, and returned to head-quarters. By the Rao, the Rani and the Nawab—the three rebel leaders now at Kalpi—the utmost efforts were put forth to render their preparations for defence as complete as possible, and their exertions, as Col. Malleson remarks, "produced one of those changes from despair to confidence which mark the Indian character." Concerning the change which took place at this time in the minds of the reassembled rebel troops, Holmes says: "Their spirits bounded from despair to the highest pitch of confidence." From an intercepted letter it was learned that the rebels were exhorted by their leaders to hold Kalpi to the end, as it was their last asylum and their only arsenal, and by exterminating the infidel English to win their right to paradise. This exhortation, which was enforced by the influence of Mahratta pundits in the neighborhood, who were preaching a crusade on behalf of the Nana's cause, had the effect to call forth a most loyal response. Moreover the position of the rebels at Kalpi, on a high bluff of the Jumna river, and surrounded on the three remaining sides by interminable ravines, was one which lent itself in a remarkable manner to defence ; and if it seemed to the rebels to be wellnigh impregnable, they might well be considered to have some show of reason for their opinion. Even beyond the ravines the rebels had extended their fortifications, expecting that the British, if not effectually checked by the defence of these outworks, would at least sustain heavy losses in attacking them there ; for the rebels had no other idea than that the British would make their attack upon Kalpi from the direction of their approach from Koonch.

But a British General of the type of Sir Hugh Rose cannot be depended on to do what the enemy expects of him. Sir Colin Campbell, the Commander-in-Chief of the army in India, well understanding how Sir Hugh's force would be reduced by exposure to the sun at the hottest season of the year in Central India, had sent a reinforcement to join him near Kalpi. This reinforcement, under the command of Col. Maxwell, was on the northern bank of the Jumna, at a village called Golowlee, six miles east of Kalpi, awaiting the coming of General Rose.

Knowing how necessary it was for every reason to gain time by as rapid a movement of his troops as possible, Sir Hugh, although time after time prostrated by sunstroke, pushed forward, not straight to Kalpi, but to Golowlee, where he knew Col. Maxwell with his force was expecting his arrival. His object in going to Golowlee was not simply to effect a junction with Col. Maxwell, but by doing this to turn the fortifications which the enemy had prepared for the purpose of obstructing his advance upon Kalpi. While thus avoiding unnecessary fighting, he would be able to attack the town in a manner wholly unanticipated by the rebels. From Golowlee as his base he had determined to make his assault. His plan was that Col. Maxwell should shell the city and fort with his batteries from the northern bank of the river, while he with his force, supplemented by Col. Maxwell's Camel Corps and his infantry, which included some Sikhs, would undertake to clear the ravines on the east side of the town, and attack the fort on its southern face.

General Rose, realising how much depended upon the issue of the battle to be fought, and anticipating that the utmost desperation would be shown by the rebels in what they would regard as their last encounter with the British, was determined that nothing should be lacking in his preparations for striking the blow that he intended should end the campaign which was fast wearing out, not only himself but all under his command. It is said that half of his troops were sick, and that all were more or less ailing. What wonder is it that such should be their case, when the mercury reached 140° at ten o'clock in the day. At this hour they were daily harassed by desultory attacks of the rebels, while the General's preparations for dealing the decisive blow were in progress. On the 21st of May, General Rose, having learned that the enemy intended to bring on a battle the next day, resolved to deliver without further delay the blow which he now felt he could safely strike.

According to expectation, at ten o'clock on the morning of the 22nd, the rebels appeared in force along the entire front of the British lines. At first they unsuccessfully attempted to mislead the British General by a feint made upon his left, while at the same time opening fire upon his centre. What occurred when the real intention of the rebels was shown is thus described by Col. Malleson:—"Suddenly, as if by magic, the whole line of ravines became a mass of fire; the enemy's left batteries opened, and their infantry, climbing from below, poured in an overwhelming musketry fire on the British right. They pressed on with loud yells, the British falling back, until the enemy approached the British light field guns and mortar battery. Then Brigadier Stuart, dismounting, placed himself by the guns, and bade the gunners defend them with their lives. The 86th and 25th Native Infantry disputed the ground step by step. Still the rebels pressed on, and it seemed as though from their numbers they must prevail, when Sir Hugh brought up the Camel Corps at their best pace; then, dismounting the riflemen, and leading them forward himself, he charged the advancing foe, who were within a few yards of the British guns. For a moment the enemy stood, but only for a moment. A shout, a dash forward from the whole British line, and the rebels went headlong into the ravines below. Thus was the victory gained. Great loss was inflicted on the rebels as they fled. Those rebels who reached the Kalpi fort felt that it was no secure place of refuge, and evacuated it in the night. The rest of their force, pursued by the horse artillery and cavalry, lost their formation and dispersed, losing all their guns and baggage."

What part the Rani of Jhansi took in this battle is not known. That she partook of the hardships of this crucial struggle there can be no doubt. She fled with the vanquished army, and when safe from her pursuers, slept under a tree.

Of what had been accomplished at Kalpi on that eventful day, Dr. Lowe wrote thus:—"A glorious victory was won over ten times our numbers under most trying circumstances. The position of Kalpi; the numbers of the enemy, who came on with a resolution and a display of tactics we had never before witnessed; the exhausted, weakened state of the General's force; the awful, suffocating hot winds and burning sun, which the men had to endure all day, without time to take food or water, combined to render the achievement one of unsurpassed difficulty."

The task which the Central India Field Force had been set to do· having been accomplished, the troops composing it began their preparations for departure to their several cantonments, glad at the prospect of well-earned rest; and their Commander was looking forward to a change to a better climate for the recuperation of his health. On the 1st of June the General's farewell order was given to his troops; whereupon they began to disperse. But almost immediately after this order had gone forth, Sir Hugh received from Col. Robertson, who had on the 25th of May been sent with a small column in pursuit of the rebels, a message to the effect that the fugitives had gone towards Gwalior. This news, if it could be true, was ominous. All doubt as to the movements of the rebels was dispelled a few hours later when another message was received by Sir Robert Hamilton confirming the tidings sent to General Rose. Action on the part of Sir Hugh was now imperative, and as soon as possible he despatched Brigadier Stuart with a portion of the first brigade to reinforce Col. Robertson. On the 4th of June the startling intelligence was received at Kalpi that not only were the rebels at Gwalior, but that Scindia's capital was in their possession. This intelligence was almost as astounding to Sir Hugh Rose and

Sir Robert Hamilton as the news of the first outbreaks of the great Mutiny had been to the British throughout India. As to what should be done there could be no doubt in the mind of General Rose, and how it should be done appeared equally clear to him. Gwalior must be recovered at once, and the task of recovering it must fall upon the troops which had composed the now disbanded Central India Field Force. Sir Colin Campbell acquiesced in this view, and telegraphed to Sir Hugh informing him that Brigadier-General Smith's brigade, which had been operating in Rajputana, and a column under Col. Riddell would join him. Sir Hugh was informed also that Brigadier-General Robert Napier was also to be sent to his assistance. The troops of the Hyderabad Contingent, which had formed a part of General Rose's force, and were on their way homeward, on hearing of the events which had occurred at Gwalior, turned back of their own accord to fight again under their old chief. As Sir Hugh now needed as large a force as he could collect, he ordered the garrison which he had left in Jhansi to march to his assistance.

But how could all this which had taken place at Gwalior have been accomplished so quickly? How was it possible for it to be accomplished at all? Who could have been the author of so bold a project?

The rebel leaders who had fought at Kalpi had fled with their followers to Gopalpore, a small town in the jungle, forty-six miles south-west of Gwalior. There Tantia Topi joined them. Could Tantia while skulking in his village have concocted the scheme of attempting to oust the Chief of the Gwalior State, who had faithfully adhered to the British, and to set up a rebel as ruler in Scindia's stead? This is by no means probable. The

Rani of Jhansi, it was thought, was the only one of the rebel leaders who was capable of devising such a plot. Of her Malleson says: "She possessed the genius, the daring, the despair necessary for the conception of grand deeds. She was urged on by hatred, by desire of vengeance, by a blood-stained conscience, by a determination to strike hard while there was yet a chance."

If that portion of Scindia's army which had not yet been disloyal to the British cause, should on the approach of the rebel army come over to its side, the taking of Gwalior would by that means be achieved. So splendid an achievement was at least possible. The plan was worthy of a trial. At the most it could only result in adding one more failure to all their other disasters.

What had been hoped for by the rebels as a possibility, was that which actually took place. The following is Malleson's account of the plan of the rebel leaders and of the meeting of the two native armies:—"The plan was to march on Gwalior with all haste, appeal to the religious and national feeling of Scindia's troops, take possession of the capital, by force if necessary, and gaining over the army of Scindia, bid defiance to the British from the rock-fortress. Emissaries were sent in the night of May 30th. Jaiaji Rao Scindia was informed that night of their arrival. The rebel force was estimated at 7,000 infantry, 4,000 cavalry and twelve guns. Scindia never wavered, though persuaded and threatened by his people. He determined to give battle to the rebels. At daybreak on June 1st he marched out with his army, and took up a position two miles east of Morar. He had 6,000 infantry, 1,500 cavalry, his body-guard of 600, and eight guns. The rebels advanced about 7 o'clock, when Scindia's eight guns opened fire. The rebels charged at a gallop and carried the guns of the opposing force. At once Scindia's infantry and cavalry deserted him, but his body-guard remained with him. When the men of the body-guard were attacked, a portion of them defended themselves with great gallantry, and did not cease fighting until many of their number had fallen. When it appeared useless to continue the contest, Scindia turned and fled accompanied by a very few of the survivors. He did not draw rein till he reached Agra. The Rani of Jhansi and her confederates entered Gwalior unopposed, took possession of the fortress, the treasury, the arsenal and the city, and began to form a government. Nana Sahib was proclaimed Peshwa, and Rao Sahib governor of Gwalior. The command of the bulk of the troops encamped outside of the city, was given to the Rani of Jhansi. Those within the city were commanded by Tantia Topi."

The plans of General Rose for marching upon Gwalior were so quickly matured that he himself with a small body of troops set out for Morar on the 6th of June, expecting to be joined on the way by other troops which under Col. Robertson and Brigadier-General Stuart had been despatched from Kalpi in pursuit of the rebels, and expecting to be further aided by the troops which were coming from Jhansi. He had issued orders to Col. Riddell to march with his column down the Agra road towards Gwalior; to Brigadier-General Smith to proceed with his brigade by the Jhansi road to Kotah-ki-sarai, five miles south-east of Gwalior; and to Major Orr, in command of the Hyderabad Contingent, to move to Paniar on the Sipri road, fifteen miles from Gwalior, in order to cut off the retreat of the rebels towards the south.

General Rose by making forced marches (for no time was to be lost, as the rainy season was near at hand) overtook Brigadier Stuart on the 12th, and reached

Bahadurpur, five miles east of the Morar Cantonment, at 6 A.M., on the 16th June. There he was joined by Brigadier-General Napier. Sir Hugh had marched his troops at night, in order that they might not suffer from the effects of the sun. Finding himself confronted by a large rebel force which might at any time make an onset upon him, he resolved, though his troops were tired, to attack at once, and Morar was taken.

Brigadier-General Smith with his brigade arrived at Kotah-ki-sarai early on the morning of June 17th. On the way he had been joined by Major Orr and his Hyderabad men, and also by the small field force from Jhansi. From his position at Kotah-ki-sarai he saw masses of rebel cavalry and infantry on the high ground between himself and Gwalior. The enemy's guns were found to be in position only 1,500 yards distant. As Brigadier Smith did not consider himself secure where he was, he determined to attack without delay. Accordingly he first sent forward his horse artillery in face of the enemy's guns, which were soon silenced. He next directed his infantry under the command of Col. Raines to follow up the attack; and this officer, employing tactics which had before been successful, ordered his men to make a rush upon the enemy on approaching near to them. The carrying out of this order had the usual effect of causing the enemy to retreat. Brigadier Smith then moved forward his cavalry. This is the description of the road which they followed, and of the fighting which ensued, as given by Col. Malleson:—"The road before debouching from the hills ran for several hundred yards through a defile. In this defile the principal fighting took place. Having gained the further end of the defile, when he joined Raines, Smith halted the infantry to guard it, and ordered his cavalry to charge. This order was most gallantly executed. The rebels, horse and foot, gave way, two guns were captured, and the Hussars continuing the pursuit through Scindia's cantonment had for a moment the rebel camp in their possession. Amongst the fugitives was the resolute woman, who alike in council and on the field was the soul of the conspirators. Clad in the attire of a man, and mounted on horseback, the Rani of Jhansi might have been seen animating her troops throughout the day. When inch by inch the British troops pressed through the pass, and when at length Smith ordered the Hussars to charge, the Rani of Jhansi fronted the British horsemen. When her comrades failed her, her horse, in spite of her effort to restrain him, carried her along with the others. With them she might have escaped, but that her horse in crossing the canal near the cantonment stumbled and fell. Then a Hussar, ignorant of her sex and her rank, cut her down. That night her devoted followers burned her body, determined that the English should not boast that they had captured her though dead."

"Whatever her faults in British eyes may have been," adds Col. Malleson, "her countrymen will ever remember that she was driven by ill-treatment into rebellion, and that she lived and died for her country."

The reader who has perused this story thus far may be interested to know something of those events which transpired at Gwalior immediately after the Rani's death, and which brought to a conclusion the military operations of Sir Hugh Rose in Central India. From the histories of Col. Malleson and Mr. Holmes the following facts have been gleaned :—

"Upon the return of the Hussars," wrote Brigadier Smith, "the officers and men were so completely exhausted and prostrated from heat and fatigue that they could scarcely sit in their saddles, and were for the movement incapable of further exertion." Smith therefore determined to content himself with holding for the night the defile and the adjoining hills on the right. The enemy, who appeared to be threatening, held their ground on the heights to the left. Col. Robertson was sent with troops to reinforce Smith, and on the afternoon of the next day General Rose, having been reinforced by the arrival of additional troops from Kalpi, marched with a portion of his force to the relief of Smith, leaving Brigadier Napier in Morar. The distance which General Rose had to traverse was long and the heat terrible. One hundred men of a single regiment were struck down by the sun. Sir Hugh bivouacked for the night on the rocky ground near Brigadier Smith's position. On the 19th at early dawn, the rebels opened a heavy fire, and Sir Hugh resolved to attack them at once. The men who had succumbed to the heat on the previous day were able to fall in with their comrades and take part in the assault. To Brigadier Stuart was committed the task of striking the decisive blow. He was directed to move forward with his infantry and crown the heights held by the enemy, while Sir Hugh himself stood ready to advance with his horse artillery, supported by the Hussars. As Stuart advanced the rebels fell back rapidly, and his infantry gave them no time to rally as they with a shout dashed over the breast works in front of them and captured the three nine-pounders with which the enemy had intended to defend that portion of the ridge. Lieut. Roome advancing at the same time with half a regiment of native infantry in skirmishing order, the other half supporting him, cleared the nearer heights, capturing two brass field-pieces and three mortars. Parties were left to guard the captured guns, while the fleeing rebels were pursued. Thus the day was won. Gwalior was practically in the hands of the British. From the position which General Rose occupied on that afternoon old Gwalior as well as the new city, with the great fortress stretching between them, stood forth clearly to view. In the plain between his position and the Lashkar were the rebel forces which had been driven from the heights. These, panic-stricken, were endeavoring to find a refuge by fleeing into one or other of the walled enclosures outside the city. The view was interesting and inspiring, and it made General Rose feel that he could take the Lashkar before sunset. He accordingly ordered a general advance. This prompt action on the part of the British Commander caused the rebels to leave on the field a large number of their guns, and abandon all idea of making a stand for the defence of the city. Pursued by the British troops which inflicted upon them great losses in killed and wounded, they retreated through the Lashkar. Left in possession of the city, General Rose at once made arrangements for its security. Thus on the 19th of June, with a loss of only eighty-seven men killed and wounded, was Gwalior retaken. That night Sir Hugh Rose rested in the regained palace of Scindia.

The great fortress was still held by a small band of rebels, who in defiance of the power which had possession of the city recommenced firing early on the morning of the 20th. Hearing the roar from the first discharge of their guns, Lieut. Rose proposed to Lieut. Waller of his regiment that they should attempt with the sepoys whom they commanded to capture the fortress. The proposition made by Rose being seconded by Waller, these two brave officers set off with their men, accompanied by a blacksmith. Creeping unobserv-

ENTRANCE OF GWALIOR FORTRESS.

ed up to the outer gateway, with the help of the blacksmith they were able without much difficulty to force this open; and with like success the remaining five gates were also thrust ajar. Not until the last gate had been thrown open did the holders of the fortress become aware of the approach of the assailants. They at once fired upon them, but the two subalterns with their sepoys dashed onwards. In the hand-to-hand struggle which ensued Lieut. Rose lost his life, but Lieut. Waller, supported by the sepoys, gained possession of the fortress.

"That day," writes Holmes, "Scindia accompanied by Sir Robert Hamilton and Charters Macpherson (who still held the office of Political Resident of Gwalior, but who, like the Maharaja of Gwalior, had been a refugee at Agra) reentered his capital. The General and a number of officers of rank went out to meet him. A squadron of the 8th Hussars, and a squadron of the 14th Light Dragoons escorted him to his palace; and the streets through which he passed were thronged by thousands of citizens who greeted him with enthusiastic acclamations."

Brigadier-General Napier had been ordered to pursue the flying rebels, and on the 22nd he overtook a large force of them at Jaora-Alipur, about twenty miles west of Gwalior. With these rebel troops were the Rao Sahib and Tantia Topi. They gave battle to their pursuer, but Napier quickly overwhelmed them, and they broke and fled, leaving all their guns (twenty-five in number), all their ammunition, their elephants, carts, tents, baggage and three or four hundred of their dead and wounded on the field. Including the guns captured at this time, the whole number of artillery pieces taken at Gwalior was fifty-two. The two surviving rebel leaders and their followers were subsequently further dealt with by Brigadier-General Napier.

With the retaking of Gwalior and the dispersion of the remnant of the rebel force on the 22nd of June the campaign of Sir Hugh Rose in Central India was finally concluded. The Major-General in once more bidding a kind farewell to the troops which had fought under him, said that he could not do so under better auspices than of the victory of Gwalior.

IX.

THE COMMITTEE'S VISIT TO JHANSI IN JANUARY, 1886.

We return now to the narration of events less exciting than those of which an account has been given in the preceding chapters—events which are but incidents connected with the beginnings of our missionary work in Jhansi,—and we do so in the belief that our readers, on account of their having first been made acquainted with the history of the place which so recently had been the theatre of such thrilling military exploits, will feel an interest not less but greater in the quieter experiences now to be chronicled.

Of the committee appointed to visit Jhansi, and report on the advisability or otherwise of its being taken up as a mission station, my husband was a member, and as we hoped to be sent to this new field, should a decision in favor of its occupancy be reached, it was thought best that I should accompany the visiting party. In order that we might take a somewhat leisurely survey of the place, my husband and I decided to go to Jhansi a day or two in advance of the other members of the committee. The journey was made by rail *via* Agra as far as Morar, where we made a brief halt at the house of our fellow-missionary, Mrs. Warren. She was greatly interested in the proposed extension of the work of the mission,

7

and as has been already remarked, had called the attention of the mission to the importance of our taking up Jhansi as one of our stations.

During our stay in Morar, Mrs. Warren, calling our attention to a passing vehicle, said, "There is the Jhansi mail-cart just leaving." This of itself would have been of little interest to us, but the mail-cart was followed by a second vehicle filled with an armed guard. We had never before anywhere in India seen anything of this kind, and it was explained that as the mail-bags had been robbed some time before between Morar and Jhansi, this armed escort had been provided to ensure their safe conveyance. Nothing could better illustrate the comparatively unsafe state of things in the heart of India before the Indian Midland Railway was completed than this picture.

Before we left Morar, a gentleman who had just paid a visit to Jhansi called at the mission house, and learning that we thought of going there to begin missionary work, asked if we had secured a house. On being told that we had not yet done so, he remarked, "I am sure you will not be able to procure even a single room to live in, as a part of the garrison now in Morar is about to be transferred to Jhansi, and every corner fit for occupancy has been engaged." This, as far as immediate requirements were concerned, was not encouraging.

On Saturday morning we continued our journey, travelling in a box-like conveyance, called a *dák gárí*, drawn by two very lean horses, which were exchanged for others equally ill-favored after we had proceeded five or six miles, and there was little or no improvement in the animals as we continued our journey. This was a fair specimen of the kind of provision made for European travellers before the days of railways. The road, however, was one of the best, being one of the principal thoroughfares of Central India.

A few miles from Morar we skirted the Lashkar, passing on the right, extensive grounds enclosed by a high stonewall. In the midst of these grounds, called *Phúl Bágh* (Flower Garden), stood the fine new palace of the Maharaja of Gwalior. Many of the people whom we passed in the vicinity of Gwalior carried arms, the most usual weapon being a short sword, a custom handed down from less peaceful times. The country between Morar and Jhansi is for the most part wild and desolate. The one walled city and the few villages which we passed on the way alleviated but little the dreariness of our journey of sixty-five miles, which was not ended until long after nightfall. Recalling the sight of the guarded mail-cart, as the daylight faded into darkness, a feeling of timidity as well as of weariness made me anxious to arrive at our destination, and it was to me no little relief to see in the moonlight the gleam of the white roads as we entered the civil station of Jhansi. After passing several residences we halted before the dák bungalow (as the travellers' rest-house is called), a long one-storied building with a veranda across the entire front. Here we were glad to find shelter and rest.

Early the following morning we looked out with interested eyes upon our surroundings. The impression was a pleasant one. From the man in charge of the rest-house we asked if there was an English church in the place. As there had long been a British Cantonment in Jhansi, it was not likely that the British soldiers quartered there would be left without a chaplain, and there was every probability that a church would also be found there.

"Yes, very near at hand," the rest-house servant replied. "What is the hour for the morning service?" we next asked. The man did not know, but said he would at once ascertain. He went off to inquire, and soon returned to say that the church service would begin at half-past ten o'clock. We accordingly went at that time, and as we entered the church, a soldier who was occupied in furnishing the pews with hymn-books, said to my husband, "You are early, Sir, as the hour for service is eleven o'clock." Seats were shown us, and as we were waiting alone in the church, the chaplain came out of the vestry. Seeing us he halted a moment, and then came forward and greeted us pleasantly. After introductions had been exchanged, the chaplain showed his friendliness by asking my husband to read the lessons for the day.

Soon after we had returned to the rest-house at the close of the service, a servant put into my hands a note from our newly-made acquaintance, inviting us to dine with him. "A traveller's bungalow," he wrote, "is, I know, a dreary place in which to spend the Sabbath. I am a bachelor, and quite alone, and it will give me much pleasure if you will dine with me this evening."

We gratefully accepted the kind invitation, and at the close of the evening service in the church, walked with our friend a short distance to his modest home. While sitting at the dinner table, our host mentioned by name some of the people of his charge who had been a help to him in his work. Among them was a judge who had been several years in Jhansi on special duty, and was about to leave. Instantly the thought came, 'It may be we shall now have a house.' When an English official is transferred from one station to another, the house he has occupied usually falls to his successor, and certain houses in a civil station are known as the commissioner's house, the collector's house, the judge's house, etc. The gentleman, whose anticipated departure the chaplain was lamenting, would not be succeeded by another, as the work he had been appointed to do would be completed at the time of his departure. There was therefore the more likelihood that we should be able to secure the house which he was about to vacate.

Early on Monday morning my husband called on the judge to ask if the bungalow he was occupying had been let to any other party. Receiving a negative reply, he next inquired who was the owner of the property, and was delighted to learn that the gentleman to whom the bungalow belonged was not only an acquaintance but a friend of ours. Of all the houses in the civil station this one then seemed to be what it has since proved to be, the one best suited to our purpose, as there was sufficient land connected with it, and it was well situated in reference to the native city. Without delay our friend was asked by telegram whether he would let his house to the mission, if when vacated by the present occupant, it should be required by us. To our joy an affirmative reply was received; and we could not but feel that our going to the church that Lord's Day morning at half-past ten instead of eleven o'clock was providential, for had we not gone at that time, we might not have met the chaplain, and might not otherwise have obtained the information, which led to our securing, at first on rent, and later by purchase, the bungalow which was to become our home.

Provisional arrangement for a house having been satisfactorily made, the remainder of Monday was spent in exploration. Wishing to pay a visit to the fort, in order that from that commanding height we might view the city and the surrounding country, we were informed that it would be necessary to obtain permission from the agent of the Maharaja Scindia, who resided in the city. This obtained, we climbed the steep ascent leading to the entrance of the fort, passed through the massive gate, and from the ramparts looked down upon the city on one side, and the English Civil Station and the Cantonment on the other. The view was very wide, and very fair. The city was well-built, and the great number of trees within the city limits formed a marked feature of the beautiful picture before us. The great amount of foliage in the inhabited area was all the more striking because of the almost total absence of trees or of verdure of any kind in the plain which stretched away beyond the city wall. Here and there we saw the domes and pinnacles of temples and the minarets of mosques. Among the humbler abodes of the people there were not wanting some stately residences, the most conspicuous of the latter being the palace whose last royal occupant was the famous Rani. In the immediate vicinity of the city were miniature lakes, and picturesque hills and crags. Standing out in bold relief we saw a rocky eminence which we were afterwards told bore the name of "Retribution Hill." The white bungalows occupied by the European residents, the barracks of the British Cantonment, and the English church were situated towards the south. The palaces and temples of the once great city of Orcha, the capital of the Bundela Kings, six miles from Jhansi, as also the castle of Burwa Sagar, twelve miles distant, could be seen. We were told that on a clear day the palaces of Datia, a walled city of 30,000 inhabitants, could also be seen. In the distance were ranges of low hills, and here and there a separate hill crowned with a ruined fortification.

The interior of the fort was in a ruinous condition.

THE CITY OF JHANSI.

A few antiquated and rusty cannons were lying about. One of the lower portions of the fort was being used as a prison. We could see the prisoners, and hear the sound of the clanking of their chains. From one of the towers of the fort fluttered the tattered ensign of the Maharaja Scindia. The fort and the high massive wall of the city bore every appearance of belonging to another age. Toward the south could be seen the breach in the wall through which the British troops forced an entrance in 1858, when Jhansi was retaken by Sir Hugh Rose. This had been but partially filled up, and to this day the battered Mamelon remains in much the same condition as when it was wrested from the rebel sepoys.

The view before us, though in many respects most interesting, was not unattended with a depressing effect, as we were looking out upon the densest heathenism, in the very centre of an idolatrous land. In this city there was not, as far as we knew, any Christian influence at work, and our subsequent acquaintance with the place proved that our surmise as to the total absence of Christian life and light in the midst of this heathen darkness was correct. As to the British residents in the Civil Station and the Cantonment, their interests, their duties and their recreations all tended to keep them aloof from the inhabitants of the native city, which was to most of them practically a *terra incognita.* That the city of Jhansi was under native rule, that it was surrounded by a wall, that aside from the peculiar architecture of its buildings it offered no attractions to those who were familiar with Indian cities, that most of the roads within the walls were unfit for wheeled vehicles, and that more or less dislike of Europeans was still felt by many of the inhabitants of the city, accounted for the fact that it was seldom if ever visited by the foreigners at its doors.

Missionaries are frequently told by those who hear from them the Gospel message, as afterwards in the Jhansi field we were told by some to whom we gave it, that they had never before heard it, but as this is often said by those who hear but do not heed, too ready credence should not be given to such declarations; for sadly true it is that many of those to whom the Gospel is preached in this land remain after their first hearing of it as destitute of the knowledge of Christ as if they had never heard His name. What is essential to the real evangelisation of the masses of Indian heathendom is that they be taught as children by those who can live among them and give them "line upon line" and "precept upon precept." This was the need which existed in Jhansi at the time of our visit, and it is safe to say that a more needy field could not be found anywhere in India.

We were thankful to know that it could not be said at the time of our coming to Jhansi, that the agents of the Furrukhabad Mission were the only persons who had ever preached the Gospel in this city. It was interesting to be told of a British government official, a Dr. B., once stationed in Jhansi, that he was accustomed to preach Christ publicly in the native city.

An instance of earnest Christian work done in Jhansi before there was a single missionary in the whole of Bundelkhand deserves special mention in this connection. Dr. James George Kemp, who entered the service of the British East India Company as an army surgeon in 1845, was in 1856 ordered to join the Irregular Cavalry at Jhansi. As he had done in other places where he had been stationed in India, so here he sought the spiritual good of all with whom he came in contact, whether Europeans, or the people of the land. At Jhansi he was the instrument used of God in the conversion of a vener-

ONE OF THE ENTRANCES TO JHANSI.

dered for the Christian faith." Mrs. Kemp closed her letter with these words concerning herself, "Would that I had known Jesus while my husband lived! It needed his death at the age of only forty years to open my eyes to opportunities lost and priceless time wasted. I had to go through a furnace of fire before my selfish life was changed. Why do I tell you all this? Only that you may see how deep an interest I feel in your work. I know that the Christless lives of our English too often check the spread of the Gospel. I cannot help much with money, but tell me if I can do anything, and remember that I am thinking of you, and will pray for you."

Before the arrival of the other members of the committee we had become quite well acquainted with Jhansi. When all had come, a survey of the situation was made by the four members of the committee collectively, and it was unanimously decided to recommend that Jhansi should by all means be occupied as a mission station, and the reasons for this decision were set forth in a paper drawn up by the senior member of the committee, the Rev. J. S. Woodside, and signed by the other members of the committee, the Rev. Thomas Tracy, the Rev. George A. Seeley, and my husband, before we left Jhansi. This paper was presented to the mission, and a copy of the same was sent to our Board in New York.

On our return journey to Allahabad we paid a visit to Aligarh, where resided the owner of the house in Jhansi, which we had secured conditionally. We wished to ascertain if the property could be purchased, in case the mission should agree to the recommendation of the committee, and our Board in America should sanction the proposed enlargement of our bounds. We found the owner of the house interested in the proposal to make Jhansi a station of our mission, but not at all anxious to dispose of his property there. "The place," he said, "will soon be an important railway centre, and in consequence the value of property in Jhansi will be greatly enhanced." He, however, told us that should the proposition to occupy Jhansi permanently be favorably received, he would sell the house to us, and the price was named, a very moderate one. He also agreed to wait until the following autumn for the decision of the Home authorities.

X.

OUR APPOINTMENT AND REMOVAL TO JHANSI.

When the paper drawn up by the committee, recommending that Jhansi be made one of our stations, was presented to the mission, opinion regarding it was divided. The depleted state of the treasury in New York, and the small hope of improvement in its condition for some time to come, led some members of the mission to feel that the proposal to extend our territory was inopportune. Others thought that as Jhansi belonged to that political division of India—the then North-West Provinces—in which lay all the stations of the Furrukhabad Mission, except Gwalior, and as it had been occupied by us as an out-station of Etawah, and had not been abandoned by the mission, although the agents who had been at work there had been withdrawn for reasons already mentioned, this field had a special claim upon us. This was the view taken by the majority of the mission, and accordingly it was decided that a missionary should be sent there without waiting for sanction from the Board, it being confidently expected that our action when explained to the Home authorities would meet with their approval.

When this decision was reached, and we had been appointed to Jhansi, we began without delay to prepare for our removal from Allahabad. Household furniture was not at that time procurable in Jhansi; it was therefore necessary that we should take with us all such articles as would be required for the furnishing of our new abode. These with our other possessions were sent by rail from Allahabad to Gwalior, and from thence were conveyed by carts to Jhansi. By this latter mode of transportation articles of furniture are especially liable to be injured, if the carts are not carefully loaded.

The loading was not therefore left entirely to the cartmen, but we gave to it our personal supervision on our arrival at Gwalior. Among the articles which we prized were some wicker chairs of Indian manufacture, especially suited to a hot climate. These we had fastened to the carts in such a way as seemed likely to ensure their safe conveyance.

At an early hour the next morning the little caravan conveying our household goods moved off from the Gwalior railway station, and we watched it a few moments as it crept slowly along the road in the direction of Jhansi. Then we returned to the mission house where we breakfasted; after which, gathering together our packages and bundles of sorts, we climbed into the clumsy *dák gári* and continued our journey.

When we had proceeded but a few miles, looking out we saw with surprise our carts drawn up together by the roadside, and the oxen, out-spanned, munching chaff most contentedly. Small fires had been kindled by the cartmen, showing that they intended waiting at this place to prepare their food for the day. They were not, however, according to custom resting on their haunches around their fires, but were reclining in free and easy fashion in our wicker chairs. Not expecting us to follow them so closely, they had thought they could safely take the opportunity to enjoy a luxury. When our conveyance came suddenly into view they were startled out of their repose, and immediately changing their programme, treated us to some very lively gymnastic exercises. These nimble Asiatics could vacate their seats in a twinkling, but as they could not so quickly replace the chairs upon the carts, these remained mute witnesses of their meddling propensities. How many other times during the journey our much-prized chairs were thus used we had no means of knowing. The value of these articles of furniture was not enhanced by such close contact with unwashed humanity.

On our arrival in Jhansi we found that the judge who occupied the house we had secured, would be unable to vacate it at the end of February, as he had expected to do, since his official duties would detain him still another month in Jhansi. It therefore became necessary that we should change somewhat the plans we had made for the month of March. It had been arranged that I should remain in Jhansi, and put our house in order, while my husband would go to Benares for a month's work with a committee engaged on the revision of the Hindi New Testament. But as that part of the programme which concerned me could not be carried out, it seemed best that I should accompany my husband. We therefore arranged for the storage of our goods until our return, and then set off on our journey to Benares.

Instead of going *via* Gwalior, we went *via* Cawnpore, though this shorter route involved a journey by *dák gárí* of twenty-four hours, covering a distance of 137 miles. A level surface, extending the whole length of our rude conveyance, was formed by covering with a board the space between the two seats, called the "well," and spreading over this surface a mattress, we were able to recline and secure a little rest at night. At distances of five or six miles our horses were changed according to custom. Sometimes the fresh animals moved off promptly; at other times they refused to stir until forced to do so by pitiless beating. We spent a weary night. A little after noon of the following day we had passed the 105th mile stone. About this time a descent in the road caused our horses to quicken their pace to such an extent that my husband began to fear for our safety, for he had previously observed that one of the wheels of our *gárí* was in an extremely rickety condition. Putting his head out of the window as quickly as possible to see whether it was likely to survive the added strain put upon it, he saw at that instant the spokes flying out of it. In consequence our conveyance overturned, but we escaped injury. When we had extricated ourselves, and the horses had been released, the driver after pausing a sufficient time to enable him fully to take in the situation, turned the heads of the animals in the direction from which we had come, and started off with them, leaving the wrecked *gárí* by the roadside.

"Where are you going?" asked my husband. The man named a town fifteen miles distant, which we had passed three hours before. "When will you return?" was next asked. "To-morrow morning," was coolly answered. For us the situation was unpleasant in the extreme. We were far from any town, and without shelter from the mid-day sun. Only the white limestone road with its dazzling glare stretched before and behind. Presently a man passed along, giving us only a glance, as if the sight was by no means an unusual one.

"Is there a bungalow anywhere in the vicinity?" asked my husband. A strange question, it seemed to me, to ask; for we were in a region, as I supposed, far from any European habitation, and I was amazed when the man answered, "Yes, *Sáhib,** just beyond that little knoll," pointing to a slight eminence but a short distance from the scene of our catastrophe, "lives Mears *Sáhib.*" Having given this information the man went on his way.

The railway line between Jhansi and Cawnpore was at this time under construction. Sections of it had been put in charge of engineers, and for their accommodation small bungalows had been built at convenient distances. It was one of these bungalows which, happily for us, was near at hand. Leaving me in charge of our possessions, my husband made his way to it. The engineer was at home, and after listening to my husband's story, replied cheerily, "You are in luck. I am about to send a construction train to Cawnpore, and I will give an order allowing you to travel by it. The railway station is two miles from here, and I will send you there in my trap." He then invited my husband to bring me over for a cup of tea.

On his return my husband found me sitting forlornly on one of our boxes shaded from the glaring sun by a large umbrella covered with white, but his face was beaming, for he had good news to communicate.

The "trap" speedily arrived, and without waiting for any refreshment we were soon on our way to the railway station. It was unfinished, but afforded shelter while we waited for the construction train to be in readiness.

Soon after we had taken our seats in one of the "wagons," the engineer and his wife passed by on a trolly. He was out inspecting that section of the line for which he was responsible. Lifting his hat when the trolly was opposite us, my husband said, "We are greatly

---

* A term of respect used in addressing Europeans or in speaking of them.

indebted to you." "Not at all, not at all; you are in luck," was the answer that floated back to us.

We reached Cawnpore in time for the train that was to convey us to the end of our journey, and with less fatigue than if we had travelled the entire distance in the conveyance in which we had left Jhansi.

As the circumstances of our sojourn in Benares were of a unique character, we shall digress briefly to relate them. Benares is the holy city of the Hindus, as Jerusalem was and still is of the Jews, and as Mecca is of the Mahomedans. There is no authentic account of its origin, for the people of India are not historians, but it is a city of great antiquity. Gautama, the founder of Buddhism, is supposed to have lived about the sixth century before Christ, and he chose this city as the centre from which to disseminate the new faith. Benares must therefore have been at that time a great and important city. It is situated on the northern bank of the river Ganges, on a bluff one hundred feet above the water. There are fifty principal flights of steps leading down to the river to facilitate bathing, for to this place come pilgrims from all parts of India to bathe in the sacred stream, hoping thus to wash away the stain of sin. Notable among the buildings on the bank of the river are the spacious residences, several stories in height, which Indian princes and noblemen have built for their own accommodation or the accommodation of their friends when on pilgrimage to the holy city. The Maharaja of Vizianagram, a South India prince, has a fine residence in Benares, not however on the river bank, but in that suburb of the city where the Europeans live. This house, which bears the name of "Windsor Castle," stands in the midst of extensive and well-kept grounds. Here its owner entertains both Indian and European guests, and here the members of the Hindi New Testament Revision Committee, who came from other cities, found a home during the time they were occupied in the work which had brought them to Benares. A sumptuous table in English style was provided, and the guests were told that they were at liberty to invite friends to take breakfast, luncheon or dinner with them whenever they desired to do so.

That a company of Christian missionaries, who were entire strangers to their royal host, who was a Hindu, should be entertained in this manner, needs explanation. Was the Maharaja interested in the work which the missionaries were doing? There was no reason to suppose that he was. His agent in Benares was deeply interested in the work of the committee, and it was at his suggestion that such generous hospitality was extended to them. The Maharaja's ready response to his agent's suggestion was nothing more nor less than pure generosity.

When at the expiration of a month, the work undertaken by the committee at this time had been completed, we returned to Jhansi. The bungalow we had rented was now vacant, and with as much expedition as possible we proceeded to put our house in order, for the heat was daily increasing.

During our absence in Benares a part of the British troops from Morar had been transferred to Jhansi, and there was great lack of house accommodation in the Cantonment. Houses were therefore sought for in the Civil Station. As soon as it became known that the house occupied by the judge was soon to be vacated, applications for it were made to the owner in Aligarh, who replied that the house had been secured by a missionary about to begin work there. In one instance at least the suggestion was made by an officer who wished if possible, to obtain the house, that we should waive our claim to it and let him have it, as he had been transferred to Jhansi by the order of the government, and must remain there. "Why not," it was asked, "postpone the beginning of your work?" We however felt that we had been sent to this city at this time by an authority higher than that of the Government of India, and that the Lord who had directed us to this place, had in a wonderful way made provision for our residence in this new field of labor. By one person the owner of the property was asked if he would dispose of it by sale. He answered that the house had been promised to us, should we desire to purchase it.

When we left Jhansi for Benares, the flag of the Maharaja Scindia floated above the fort. On our return, the British flag waved there. Never on any occasion in any land, had our hearts more rejoiced when we had seen the Stars and Stripes, the flag of our own beloved land, floating in the breeze, than now when we saw the Union Jack, waving above the grey old fort. We knew that it meant protection not only for the European subjects of Her Majesty the Queen of England and Empress of India, but justice for the humblest among her Indian subjects. A new and brighter day had dawned for the city whose record had been so dark.

XI.

BEGINNING AT THE FIVE WELLS.

The six hottest months of the year—April to September inclusive,—months the least favorable for evangelistic efforts of any kind, were spent in Jhansi. We entered upon our new field unaccompanied by helpers, and for this reason also we were not able to accomplish during these first months in Jhansi all that otherwise might have been done. Nevertheless a beginning was made. And I am now to tell how I found the first opening for work among the women of Jhansi.

The *Panch Kúe* or Five Wells of Jhansi are famed not only for the inexhaustible supply of water which they furnish, but also for the excellence of this element so essential to life and comfort. These wells, which are in close proximity to one another, are situated in an open space on one side of the city, and are the property of the Municipality. Not only do the city authorities allow free access to these wells, but facilities for drawing the water are supplied without charge. The morning is the favorite time for visits to these wells, and troops of Rebeccas with their water-pots on their heads, going to or returning from the wells, may any day be seen. The water of these wells is carried to all parts of the city, and it is said that the number of women who go daily to the *Panch Kúe* for their water supply is not less than one thousand.

THE FIVE WELLS.

My husband returned from a walk in the city one morning greatly elated with the discovery which he had made of these wells, and his face beamed with pleasure as he described them and their surroundings to me. Facing the main entrance to the open area, where the wells were, was a large temple. Grand old *pípal* trees, regarded as sacred by the Hindus, shaded the place. Around the immense wells were gathered groups of women who had come to draw water. Each one possessed a rope or cord with which she lowered her vessel to the water and drew it up when filled. The whole scene—the white temple, the fine trees, the women busy at their tasks, many of whom were clothed in bright raiment—formed, my husband told me, one of the most picturesque sights he had witnessed in India.

Here, we both felt, was my opportunity, and early one morning soon after this, with my husband as my guide, and well supplied with illustrated papers in Hindi, I made my way to these wells. It was a novel and an intensely interesting scene upon which I looked. Around the wells, each from sixteen to eighteen feet in diameter, were gathered many women, not servants merely, but evidently women of the households, not a few of whom were well dressed and decked with ornaments. They came and went, a constant procession, bringing their empty vessels upon their heads, and bearing them away in the same manner, with a freedom of motion and grace of carriage that a princess might envy. Usually each woman carried upon her head two water-pots, one above the other, the upper one resting upon the mouth of the one below it, while the lower one was poised upon a ring made of twine placed upon the head. How with such a weight resting upon them they can maintain so erect a position, and how they can preserve so even a balance when walking, and chatting together as they walk, is ever a wonder to us, as we observe them.

When my husband had withdrawn in order to make it easier for me to approach the women, they began, one and all, to view me with wondering curiosity. I sought to win their confidence by saying a pleasant word to one and another, and at length I offered to one of them one of the prettily illustrated papers which I had with me. One woman who ventured near shook her head, but another timidly stretched forth her hand, took the proffered gift, and after showing it to some others, carefully wrapped it in one corner of her *chaddar*,* then lifted her water-jars to her head and walked away. Others then came forward for the papers, and not women only, but priests from the temple.

I continued to visit the five wells, and through these visits and the papers given to the women the truth which we desired to disseminate reached many homes. As I passed to and fro the people began to recognise me and to watch for my coming. It was pleasant as I looked into some face pressed against an opening in a doorway to meet an answering smile. But I longed to enter these homes, to sit down among the women and tell them of Jesus. When I least expected it, God sent a helper to be a pioneer for me in the zenanas of this city.

One day a native Christian woman called at our bungalow with her son, a young man employed in one of the government offices in Jhansi. She told us that she had worked for several years as a Bible-woman in Agra, and that she had now come to spend a few months with her son. She was willing to take employment with me, and was at once engaged.

---

* A cloth used as a covering for the upper part of the body and as a veil for the head.

WOMEN CARRYING WATER JARS.

Through this helper, Catharine by name, an entrance was soon obtained for me into some of the houses in the city. While teaching one day in a house where the women seemed unusually friendly, the Bible-woman said, "I know a foreign lady who loves the women of India, and who would be pleased to visit you." "Is she the lady we have seen at the wells?" was at once asked. "The very same," was Catharine's answer. "Then you may bring her," was the reply given without hesitation.

At another time as we were passing a certain house, we noticed a number of women gathered about the door smiling and nodding, and I said to Catharine, "Do you visit this house?" "Not yet," she answered, "but they are beginning to know me, and I shall soon be invited to go there to teach." Thus door after door was opened to us.

Once while visiting a house in which several women from houses in the immediate vicinity had gathered to meet us, the announcement was made that the master of the house had returned from his office. Fearing that he might be annoyed at finding so many people in his house, I rose to take leave, but the wife laid a detaining hand upon my arm, and in a persuasive voice said, "Do not go yet; the *Bábú* is pleased to have you here."

A score or more of houses were at length opened to us, and in these we were cordially received. The women who gathered about us in these homes listened with interest to the reading of Bible narratives and such little books as unfolded in simple language the truth of the Gospel, and they never wearied of the singing of Christian songs, though to ears attuned to melody Catharine's rendering of these would have been torture. Happily the women were able to separate the sentiment from the unmusical accompaniment, and would sometimes sit with tears streaming down their cheeks, and uttering such ejaculations as "How true! how true! what a picture of the lives we lead, hopeless and full of sorrow!"

Catharine objected to the drudgery of teaching the women to read. "Preaching," as she styled her attempts at instruction in things sacred, was to her a much more congenial occupation. We had, however, one pupil so eager to learn to read that teaching her was no drudgery even to unwilling Catharine. We met her one day in a house we had often visited. She was a high-caste widow, with an attractive face and manner. She listened with great interest to the instruction given to her friend, and as we were leaving, said to us, "Will you not come and teach me?" "With pleasure," we answered; "next week when in this neighborhood we will come to your house." "Come to-day," she urged; "not to give me a lesson, for it is already late, but that I may show you where I live. You may not be able to find the house alone."

She would not be denied, and we followed her through many a narrow street before we reached her house. "You will be sure to come next week; you will not forget," she pleaded, as we turned away. We did not forget, and we found her waiting to welcome us. She took us into an inner room, and with her fatherless little boy sitting on the mat beside her, and her book spread open before her, her fingers followed the letters some of which she already knew, and in a low musical voice she went on with her lesson, apparently regardless of the presence of a tall, stern-visaged woman who hovered about, and who seemed to possess within her the elements of a small hurricane, the surcharged spirit finding relief in the slamming of doors, the dropping of heavy articles, and the occasional uplifting without provocation of a voice tremulous with wrath. This creature sustained to our new pupil a relationship which in an Indian household is by no means synonymous with motherly tenderness. She was the mother-in-law.

For some time we continued our visits to this interesting pupil, whose eagerness to learn, and whose rapid progress made us willing to face her mother-in-law, though the wrath of this churlish woman appeared to gather strength in proportion to the comfort which the gentle daughter-in-law seemed to draw from our visits. We tried to propitiate her, but our advances were coldly received. Reaching this house one day in our round of visits, we were told at the entrance, that our pupil had gone to a distant village to visit a relative. Whether this was true or not we had no means of ascertaining. Whatever the fact was, we were never again permitted to see her. It was a sore disappointment, but alas! not an uncommon experience in our work.

Among the members of another household which we visited, we learned to feel a peculiar interest in a blind daughter, a woman in middle life. Whenever we went to this house, women from the adjoining houses flocked in. They would sit silent and attentive until some trivial interruption occurred, which never failed to divert their thoughts from the lesson; but our blind pupil with her hands folded across her lap, and her face turned toward the speaker, remained to the end of the lesson almost motionless. When questions were asked concerning the instruction given, she was the first to answer. As is usual with the blind she possessed a remarkably retentive memory. In the singing of Christian songs she took great delight. This blind daughter, so quiet and gentle, and attentive to the instruction given, was as different as possible from her bustling mother, who never sought in any way to hinder our teaching, but whose mind seemed engrossed with family cares and neighborhood gossip to the exclusion of any aspiration for things higher and better.

The Hindi handbills and illustrated papers which I was accustomed to take with me, not only to the Five Wells, but to the houses visited, were very much sought after, and women who could not read, frequently asked for them for sons who at school had learned to read.

In several of the families visited, there were bright lads who could read well. They were always pleased to see us, and listened with interest to the lesson given, enjoying especially the questioning which followed, as it gave them an opportunity to show by their answers how well they understood the instruction given, and how much of it they remembered. Simple tracts, such as "The Story of Love," and "The Lost Sheep," were in great request. Frequently one of these tracts was read through at a visit, and sometimes the reader was a boy belonging to the family visited. To see her son thus honored was always a great delight to the mother, who listened to the reading with beaming face, while glancing now and then at the visitors to see if they fully appreciated the attainments of her cherished boy. Some of the booklets were so frequently read that the women were able to repeat from memory the entire story, the lessons of which they readily grasped. Mothers frequently asked for an illustrated paper or a leaflet to send to an absent son, and if a book was asked for, the price was gladly given.

Catharine remained with us for about a year, and not long after the expiration of this period we were able to place the zenana teaching on a better footing by employing a European teacher of long experience, funds for the purpose having been most opportunely and in a wonderful manner providentially provided.

XII.

FIRST TOUR AMONG THE VILLAGES.

The work which called my husband to Benares in the spring made it necessary that he should be absent from home for more than a month during the autumn of our first year in Jhansi. This time the New Testament Revision Committee met in Naini Tal, in the Himalaya mountains. It was a part of my husband's duty as Secretary of this Committee to make arrangements for the entertainment of its members, and as I could materially assist in this department, I accompanied him. The commencement of our acquaintance with our field outside the city of Jhansi was therefore delayed until near the close of 1886.

There is much to be done in preparation for even a short tour in the district. Our dwelling must usually be a tent. The necessary articles of camp furniture are made to fold, in order that they may be more easily packed and transported. Cooking utensils, table furniture and articles of food must be provided. A small stock of such medicines as can safely be administered by a non-professional, in most cases forms a part of the outfit of a missionary when entering upon a tour, as by the use of simple remedies such as cough mixture, quinine, linament, etc., he may relieve physical suffering and thereby gain a more friendly hearing for the Gospel message. Christian books and tracts, including, of course, the Bible and Scripture portions, are always carried with us, as the printed page finds its way into homes where the missionary may not be allowed to enter.

Exploration was one object of our first tours in the district, and these sketches of our itinerations are written partly for the purpose of enabling others to see through our eyes what we saw from day to day. We hope therefore that our descriptions of the places which we visited, and of the people among whom we moved, may serve to enable our readers to behold with some degree of vividness the scenes which to us, as we first beheld them, were so full of interest.

We left home on the morning of the 22nd of December in a light two-wheeled conveyance, and drove to the old ruined city of Orcha, a distance of six miles. Two carts laden with camp equipage had been despatched on the previous day. Arriving at the site on which once stood the populous Bundela capital, we passed through an arched gateway which may have been one of the avenues by which the walled city was entered. If this was the case, we were doubtless following the road trodden of old by the common people; for at a short distance from this avenue was a far more imposing entrance which had all the appearance of having been the royal road.

A large portion of the city wall, constructed of boulders, is still standing and is from eighteen to twenty feet high. We drove for a considerable distance over rough ground, in appearance not unlike the ground outside the wall, and at length our road led through a narrow, inhabited street, beyond which we came out upon an open space near the river Betwa, where we found our encampment. Before us rose two stately palaces, which though they have been greatly neglected, still remain in a good state of preservation. The

PALACES AT ORCHA.

grounds connected with these palaces are surrounded by a wall of solid masonry, past which, toward the south, flows the "withy-covered" stream, as its Sanskrit name, Vetravati, signifies. Nothing resembling the willow is, however, now to be found along the banks of the beautiful Betwa, but it is said that the kind of reed which gave to this stream its name, is still to be seen at its source in the Vindhya mountains not far from Bhopal. At all times of the year, except the rainy season, the Betwa is but a shallow stream, and yet the quantity of pure limpid water which flows perennially over this river-bed throughout its whole extent of 340 miles is so considerable, that one cannot help wondering that springs affording such inexhaustible supplies should exist in the mountains of Central India. The British Government by constructing the great canal which is fed by the Betwa river and used to irrigate a large extent of arid country, has taken measures to prevent the water of this stream from running to waste.

On the bank of the river at Orcha, at a short distance from the palaces, are the mausoleums of the Bundela kings. These are stately structures, the most imposing one being the mausoleum of Bir Singh Deo. These mausoleums are also *suttee* monuments, and probably mark the spots where the widows of the kings were burned alive with the dead bodies of their husbands. Beyond the boulder-strewn river-bed stretches a dense jungle, and in the distance are seen low ranges of hills, which are a characteristic feature of the scenery of Bundelkhand.

As my husband had no Hindustani helpers of his own, two preachers belonging to another station were kindly lent to him for this tour. On the first evening after our arrival in Orcha, the missionary and his helpers went into the town, said to contain a population of about two thousand people, who are scattered here and there among the ruins, to see if an audience could be gathered to listen to the Gospel story.

I was thus left alone, and darkness came on before the preachers returned. Standing in the tent door and looking out, I saw above me the heavens studded with stars, while not a single taper glimmered from the massive piles before me. The gloom in which the palaces were enshrouded was a fit emblem of the spiritual darkness which had brooded over this capital in the days of its kings, and which to a very great extent still covers this whole land.

On the morning following our arrival, while my husband and his assistants were engaged in preaching, I made my way to the great temple—the largest in North India. This temple stands on a somewhat elevated base of rock. It has a lofty central dome, and groups of towers elaborately carved. It is built in the form of a Greek Cross, the arms being united by the central dome. The interior has fallen into disrepair, for long ago ceased alike the royal patronage, and the offerings of throngs of worshippers, which served to maintain its inward splendor. The local celebrity of this temple, however, is still preserved by a yearly festival, when occurs a general exodus of the Hindu population of the city of Jhansi for the purpose of worshipping at this shrine. A few priests still linger about the old temple. One of these, wrapped in his blanket, was sleeping in an alcove. Another emerged from an inner room, looking almost as ancient and dilapidated as did the temple. On the stone pavement under the dome a fire had been kindled, and over the embers a little group were crouching. The

GREAT TEMPLE AT ORCHA.

figure in the alcove shook himself out of his blanket, and joined the group around the fire, shivering as he stretched out his hands over the coals, though outside the sun was shining gloriously, and shedding a genial warmth. In another corner of the temple a venerable priest was baking thin cakes of bread over a fire, and as I passed by he cried out, "Don't come near me," fearing lest my shadow falling on his food should defile it.

The palaces are connected with the town by a massive stone bridge, thrown over a channel into which, during the rainy season, extends an arm of the river. Making the round of the palaces one morning we noticed that the custodians passed without opening for us some of the upper rooms, and when we inquired the reason for this, they replied, "These rooms are devoted exclusively to the use of the ladies of the Raja's household. When they depart, the Raja himself seals the doors, and no hand but his ever breaks the seals." From one of the towers we had a magnificent view of river and fort-crowned hills. Dimly in the distance could be seen the fort of Jhansi. To this ancestral capital the Raja of Orcha occasionally comes from Tehri with a great retinue, and on such occasions the palaces are again pervaded with an air of festivity, and for a brief period the ruins wake from their slumber. A grand gala-day for Orcha was the occurrence of a recent visit to this place by the present Governor-General of India, Lord Curzon.

The present head of the Orcha State is among the most enlightened of the princes of Central India. It was lately said in his praise that he was "conspicuous for his loyalty, his liberality, and an earnest desire to rule for the good of his people." In recognition of his distinguishing characteristics, the British Government has conferred on him the title of "The first of the Rajas of Bundelkhand." Upon the Governor-General's Agent for Central India devolved the duty of investing this Prince with the new honor, and in the old capital the Raja, accompanied by a large number of nobles and headmen richly dressed, and attended by a multitude of retainers, received the representative of the Imperial Government. A large company of guests from Jhansi and the neighboring cities were invited to witness the investiture. Tents for the reception of the guests were pitched on the bank of the river. The durbar was held in one of the palaces. At the conclusion of the imposing ceremony the Raja received his guests in a large and handsome durbar tent, and by his side were his two sons, of whom he is very proud. The usual festivities followed, and when these were concluded, all departed, and Orcha was left once more to its silence and its gloom.

On the morning of December 24th we struck tents at Orcha, and sending our carts to Barwa Sagar, the place of our next encampment, drove back to Jhansi for some necessary articles, and to get our mail. We spent the night in our bungalow, and drove to Barwa Sagar, twelve miles distant, the following morning. Rarely have we seen in India a more lovely scene than that upon which our eyes rested on our arrival at our new camp. Our tents had been set up on a high embankment overlooking a beautiful artificial lake. On the shores of the lake were green fields, and in the distance were ranges of hills, while nearer at hand were picturesque rocky eminences. Overlooking the lake, rose the stately castle of Barwa Sagar. There were grand old trees on the embankment and below it. In no more charming spot had we ever passed a Christmas, and with hearts overflowing with gratitude for all the way

THE EMBANKMENT AT BARWA SAGAR.

in which God had led us, we sat down to our table in our tent. Against a low wall a rude cooking-range had been built of stones and mud, and from a limited store of provisions a savory dinner had been prepared.

It was delightful as the day was closing to watch the effect of the sunset upon the placid lake. The beauty of the surrounding country contributed greatly to the enchanting scene, while the grand old castle near by reminded us that we were on historic ground.

My husband and his co-workers went into the town after dark to meet the people. They took with them a sciopticon and exhibited a number of Bible pictures, upon which a large audience gazed with delight while they listened to the explanation given by the preachers. The next day we visited a school for boys, and gave Gospel leaflets in Hindi to all who could read. Night after night large crowds gathered around the preachers and listened with eager interest to their message, which the magic-lantern helped to impress upon their minds. The most favorable time for meeting the people, and in fact almost the only time when the villagers can be gathered together in any considerable number to listen to the preaching, is after nightfall. The work of the day being over, and the evening meal having been eaten, they are then at leisure. Singing always attracts them, and most of our preachers are able to sing well enough to please a village audience.

Barwa Sagar is a well-built town of 6,000 inhabitants, and we were impressed with its prevailing air of thrift. In a previous chapter mention was made of the lakes of Bundelkhand as forming a distinguishing feature of this part of India. It was a delightful experience to discover a number of these lakes as we proceeded on our tour, for before we started we were ignorant of the existence of any of them except the lake of Barwa Sagar. This lake is one of the largest, and is also one of the most beautiful of the great artificial reservoirs for which the eastern part of the Jhansi district is noted. Its embankment, nearly three-fourths of a mile long, is a work of art. Throughout its whole extent stone steps descend in zigzag form to low water-mark, producing a fine effect. The word Sagar means sea, and the great reservoir is fed by a stream called the Barwa, from which it derives its name. Under the beneficent rule of the British, the waters of this lake and of other lakes in Bundelkhand, are no doubt a greater blessing than formerly, for now they are sent forth in fertilising streams over wide areas. To its lake the town of Barwa Sagar owes its abundant and uninterrupted prosperity. Here the tillers of the soil seldom if ever have to reckon with drought and consequent famine, which not unfrequently have been so great a scourge in this part of the country. In the large government garden near the lake we found magnificent clusters of the tall feathery bamboo, long rows of plantains, and other tropical productions. The native gardener in charge sent to our tent after our arrival a present of fruit and vegetables, together with a bouquet of violets, whose delicate perfume carried us back in memory to a land beyond the seas.

Our third camping-place was ten miles from Barwa Sagar, on the side of the beautiful Arjar lake. On the embankment, in a position which afforded a view of the entire sheet of water and its surroundings, our tent was set up. This embankment was constructed in the 17th century by one of the Orcha Rajas. Nine villages in the neighborhood of this lake were visited by the preachers. Now and then a fisherman's tiny boat glided over the glassy surface of the water. Some excellent fish were

SUGAR-CANE PRESS AT BARWA SAGAR.

brought to us on the morning of our arrival. On the following morning the fishermen again appeared, but with empty nets, telling us that they had plied their craft all through the night, but fruitlessly. Very vividly did this bring to our minds those fishermen of Galilee, who said to Jesus, " Master, we toiled all night and took nothing."

The preachers strove to make Christ known to the people with whom they here came in contact, but they were deeply impressed with the fact that the evangelisation of these darkened souls would not be the work of a day or a week. They found these simple villagers exceedingly friendly and hospitable. They were ever ready to give my husband water or milk to drink, and even a Brahman did not scruple to offer him drink in his own vessel. Indeed among the people of this region it is no uncommon thing for the missionary and his helpers after they have preached in a village to be invited to remain a little longer in order that food may be prepared for them. This is especially noteworthy, as it was unlike any thing they had experienced in any other district.

When it became known that we had tracts and books in Hindi, numbers of lads came from the different hamlets across the lake to get them, and returned much pleased with their new possessions, to obtain which they had parted with their hard-earned pennies. It was pleasant to find so many persons, old and young, who could read and write. When afterwards we examined the census returns of the government, we found that the district of Jhansi had a larger percentage among the male population able to read and write, calculated on the number of boys in the age group of five to nine years, than any other district occupied by our mission. This was cheering; for as readers multiply, the circulation of the Scriptures, and of Christian literature will increase.

On the last day of the year we moved ten miles further on. The scenery along the road to our new camp was much enjoyed, the contrast between the rugged hills on every side, and the well-cultivated fields being very striking. It was the time when the crops needed irrigation, and water for this purpose was being raised from shallow wells by means of the Persian wheel. We could have pitched our tent beside another lake in one of the most picturesque of spots, the entrance to the camping-ground being between giant crags, which stood like sentinels at a gap in a low range of hills. The camping-ground itself was shaded by gigantic trees. The place was in every respect an ideal one for a few days' sojourn under canvas, but we chose to pass by the lake, and take up our abode in a building which appeared to have been at one time a temple, but which by additions made to it had been converted into a rest-house for government officials chiefly, any traveller, however, being at liberty to use it for a temporary shelter. Here the new year found us comfortably settled, green fields of grain surrounding us on all sides. A flight of steps conducted us to an upper terrace of our dwelling, and from this another flight led to the top of a tower which commanded a prospect of rare loveliness.

One of the days which we spent here was the Lord's Day, and in the large upper room of our habitation we held our Christian service. Early in the morning of this day my husband had a very interesting meeting in a neighboring village, where in a room of one of the houses a goodly number of men listened most attentively while he discoursed to them of the coming to this world of man's Redeemer, of his life on earth, and of his death on our behalf. At the close of this meeting one of the listeners said, "I have a book which tells all about this";

and then at my husband's request he brought it to show to him. It was the *Susamáchár* (Good News)—the New Testament in Hindi. He had bought it at a *melá* (religious festival) in Allahabad. Thus the Word of God in printed form had preceded the visit of the missionary, and thus it finds its way to many places which the missionary never visits.

As in our former encampments, we found the people very friendly, and we were often touched by the confidence which they placed in us as physicians, for by the village people all Europeans are supposed to know more or less of the healing art. One day a woman, bent and withered, came with a younger woman of her household, to ask if we could do anything for her eyes, for she was losing her sight. A fisherman showed my husband a sightless eye, explaining that he had lost it by an accident when making his boat, and asked if it could be restored. Was it not precisely thus that many came to Jesus in the days when he was an itinerant missionary? And we read that they did not come in vain.

We drove one afternoon to a small hamlet which lay at the foot of the hills a mile or more distant, our object being to see a settlement of aborigines, of whom there are 10,000 in the Jhansi district. In those parts of India where numerous converts have been won for Christ, they have usually been from among the low caste people, or from the aboriginal tribes who have no caste, and are not properly classified as Hindus. The aborigines in this district are not cultivators of the soil, and do comparatively little work for their Hindu neighbors. They subsist chiefly on what they are able to gather from the forest. On the day of our visit we found only women, children, and old men in the hamlet, the able-bodied members of the community having gone to the other side of the hill to cut bamboos. Their dwellings were small huts, whose framework was formed of branches of trees, and whose covering was composed of twigs and leaves. When we inquired what they worshipped, a hideous image painted in vermilion, and leaning against the trunk of a tree, was pointed out to us. What else should they do but what the Hindus did?

As we drove away from Kachneo on the morning of the third of January, we turned back to catch yet another glimpse of the fair scene. A drive of six miles brought us to our next camping-place, the town of Ranipur. We went at once to the post-office, hoping to find our American letters. A postman, we were told, had just gone out with a package for us, and was searching for our camp. We pitched our tent on a triangular plot of ground between two roads, and under the shade of some fine trees. Here our letters reached us.

Ranipur is a town of 6,000 people, with clean streets and many well-built houses. The chief object of interest in the town is a very costly and handsome Jain temple. Soon after our arrival a native official, accompanied by a train of attendants, presented himself, and asked how he could serve us. We made known our wants, which were promptly supplied, for "a consideration," of course, and our camp was soon in order. In the evening the preachers went forth, and with the aid of the sciopticon soon gathered an interested audience. The following morning, soon after my husband returned to the camp from his second visit to the town, boys and young men began to come for books. They were thoroughly wide-awake and anxious to drive a hard bargain. Before the close of the day all the Gospel portions in our stock had been exhausted, not because of regard felt for the

WITH SOME ABORIGINES.

Word of God, for it was a new book to them, but the large, clear type attracted the eager purchasers, and they were pleased to get a large number of pages for a comparatively small price. There was in the town a government school for boys with seventy pupils in attendance, which fact accounted for the ready market found for our books.

"I want Looke," meaning the Gospel of Luke, some of the boys said, as they came to buy, while others repeated the titles of some of our standard tracts as glibly as if they had long been familiar with that kind of literature. While my husband was preparing to go out in the evening, two men came from the town to ask if he would not talk to them again. He accompanied them, and a large audience soon gathered and listened attentively to the addresses given. Greatly to our regret we were obliged to move on to our next halting-place on the following day, as our time was limited, and in the early morning we drove to Mau, five miles distant from Ranipur.

Mau is a flourishing market town of 16,000 inhabitants, with busy streets, and many large and handsome buildings. Its bazaars are as fine as those of many larger cities. It is situated between two rivers, one of which we crossed as we entered the place. Not finding in the immediate vicinity of the town a convenient and desirable place for an encampment, we drove out two miles and pitched our tent in a pleasant grove, where was a good well, an important consideration when choosing a locality for a camp. At sunset ominous clouds gathered in the west, and we soon heard the noise of thunder. At midnight we were aroused by the sound of a mallet striking heavily upon the stakes to which the cords of our tent were fastened. The stakes were being driven deeper into the ground, to prevent our tent from being blown over by the wind, whose violence was rapidly increasing. Soon the rain descended in torrents, and the storm continued for several hours. At daybreak our camp looked dismal enough, but the sun struggled through the clouds before the morning had far advanced, and in consequence, the dreariness with which the day began, soon disappeared, and every thing again wore a cheerful aspect.

In the afternoon we drove to the town and visited a school for boys. As at Ranipur, so here the schoolboys were eager to obtain our books, many of which were left in their possession. We found that the heavy rainfall of the previous night had swept away the river-crossings, and that consequently the only approach to the town then open, was the one by which we had come from our camp. This made us appreciate our position more than ever, for had we pitched our tents on the usual camping-ground on the other side of the river, we should have been entirely cut off from the town, and our work would have been at a standstill. As it was, the storm and the dampness which it occasioned hindered considerably our out-of-door preaching.

During one of the days spent in Mau while I was with my husband in the town, two little sons of one of the native officials came to make their salaams to us. They were handsome boys, richly dressed, and very polite in demeanor. An oriental is an adept in the art of concealing his feelings. You cannot tell how much weight to attach to his words, and you will search in vain to find through any change in his countenance the key to his heart. He begins in childhood his lessons in self-control. As the sons of the official stood beside us, attended by their servant, some one in the company, pointing to the younger of the two brothers, said, "That boy is wonderfully clever." We looked at the child, apparently about eight years of age, to see what effect this flattery would have upon him, but he seemed as one who did not hear. Just then a wandering musician appeared upon the scene, having with him a boy ten or eleven years of age. After making a low obeisance, this boy began to sing. He had a voice of peculiar sweetness, and his slender fingers swept the strings of his instrument with no mean skill. He did not deign to cast even a glance toward the handsomely dressed children, and they in their self-contained importance and imperturbable equanimity, ignored both him and his music, and made their adieus in the middle of his performance.

On our return journey we travelled as far as Barwa Sagar by the macadamised road, which runs parallel to the mud road by which we had gone to Mau. This enabled us to visit additional villages on our way back to Jhansi. At the end of each stage we found comfortable rest-houses, which we were glad to occupy, as our stay in each place was short. Arriving at a post-town at the end of our second stage we found a packet of American letters and papers awaiting us. The postal arrangements in India deserve special mention, because they are exceptionally good. Even when frequently changing camps in the district, letters are seldom lost. They follow the traveller from place to place, and are delivered by postal peons, who not unfrequently walk long distances in the discharge of their duty. At Barwa Sagar, as it was necessary for us to limit our stay to one day, we lodged in the old castle, from which we enjoyed magnificent views on all sides. Another visitor was there, an army surgeon, who had come out for a day's shooting. We watched his little boat as it skimmed over the lake, and heard occasionally the report of his rifle. When he returned to the castle, he bore proudly, as the result of his morning's "sport," a fine bag of game. The English are a sport-loving people, which fact largely accounts for the physical force which they are able to maintain even in the debilitating climate of India.

The mention of this officer recalls another, from whom, as he had visited Barwa Sagar, we inquired before starting on this tour, as to whether there was a village or town near the lake. He had not seen a village there, and was doubtful about the existence of one. As a matter of fact, he had seen nothing there except the castle in which he had lodged, and the lake which afforded him the sport which he desired. And yet there was a large town close to the castle. This well illustrates how people see those things which they have eyes to see, and are blind to all else. This is true of European residents in India who have an opportunity of seeing for themselves the missionary work which is being carried on here. According to their predilections, they see or do not see what the missionaries are doing in this land. One interested in missions will be able to tell of Christian communities and Churches, and of various evangelistic and philanthropic agencies which have come under his observation; while another who has felt no interest in missions, and consequently has had no eyes to see what others have seen, will perhaps be only too ready by his remarks upon the subject to throw doubt upon the matter of missionary success. Would that it were better understood that those who have nothing good to say of the missionary work, as well as those who speak in appreciation of it, do by what they say most distinctly reflect their own individual character.

The Gospel was preached in the town of Barwa Sagar in the evening of the day we spent there, and on the following morning we drove to Jhansi. During this tour

BARWA SAGAR CASTLE AND LAKE.

of twenty-two days we pitched our tents in eight different places, made brief halts at three other places, and twenty-three towns and villages were visited, some of them on two or three different occasions.

XIII.

FIRST HELPERS SENT TO US, AND FURTHER TOURING IN THE DISTRICT.

In June 1887 we were gladdened by the arrival of our first helpers, the Rev. E. Nabibakhsh and his wife. He had been a valued laborer in Etawah, but with the consent most generously given of the missionary at that station, and the sanction of the mission, he and his wife were transferred to Jhansi. This brother did not come as a stranger to this field, for, as has been related, when Jhansi had been an out-station of Etawah, he was one of those sent to begin the work here, and was the leader of the pioneering party. A man in middle life, he had an honorable record, and we were thankful to have such a helper sent to us. He had been in the care of the mission from his boyhood, having been received as an orphan, and had been educated at Fatehgarh. In this connection I will add nothing more concerning him, as an account of his eventful boyhood and subsequent career will be given in the following chapter. The wife of our helper, also received as an orphan child, had been brought up and educated in the mission. She had been in my care for a time at Allahabad, and was afterwards sent by us to our orphan school in Fatehgarh. She grew into a fine woman, and was eventually married to the minister who became our first fellow-worker in Jhansi.

On their way to us they had travelled from Etawah to Gwalior by rail, and from Gwalior to Jhansi by a common country cart. We had expected them on Saturday, but they did not arrive on that day, and we had begun to feel anxious about them when on Sunday morning they appeared at our door. The cause of their delay was the breaking down of the cart in which they had started from Gwalior. When thus halted in their journey they were far from any shelter, and they were obliged to wait by the roadside until from a distant village another cart could be procured. "Happily there was a well at hand," said the minister, "and this was a great boon to us, as the heat was very great, and besides there was still some food in our basket which we had brought from Etawah, and with this we could refresh ourselves."

There were on the mission premises no houses which could be used for the accommodation of our helpers; and furthermore, when beginning work in our new station we had resolved not to introduce the "compound system," as it is called, that is, the plan of colonising the Christian community on mission ground outside the native city. The reason for this was that when converts from heathenism or Mahomedanism live under the shadow of a missionary, a spirit of dependence prejudicial to manliness of character is apt to be engendered in them; and also that when living apart from the non-Christian community, they have less opportunity of exerting a Christian influence upon it.

The brother who had been sent to us had been inured to self-reliance, and moreover, chiefly in this very city of Jhansi had been schooled in self-dependence. He therefore unhesitatingly set about to find in the native city a house in which he and his family could live. His quest was, to our joy, successful, but it was not without some difficulty that a house in the city was secured, owing to the large influx at this time of newcomers attracted hither by the great amount of work of all kinds which was being carried on in connection with railway construction. The great demand for house accommodation in the old city at the time of our beginning work in Jhansi may be inferred from the fact that during the first five years of our residence in this new station, its population increased from 32,000 to 52,000.

The house which was secured was in the very heart of the city, and there our co-workers were soon comfortably domiciled. They soon made the acquaintance of the people in the immediate vicinity of their new home, and the pleasant manners of the Christians made an ever increasing circle of friends for them. It was in an upper room of this house, a room measuring about eight by ten feet, and furnished with two chairs and a bench, that we began our Sabbath service. In the open court below we had a Sunday-school. The attendance was small, but it served to make us known. The door of the house, left hospitably open, was an invitation to any one to enter, and the singing of hymns in the vernacular always proved an attraction.

Before the cold season of 1887-88 had passed, accompanied by the Rev. Nabibakhsh, we visited some of the chief centres of population north and north-east of Jhansi, spending in this way nearly five weeks. At the distance of only seventeen miles from Jhansi, towards the north, is the city of Datia, the capital of a native principality, ruled by a Bundela chief. According to the census of 1881 this city had more than 28,000 inhabitants, and the principality contained a population numbering nearly 180,000. At the commencement of

HOUSE OF REV. NABIBAKHSH.

this season's touring we were attracted by these thousands of souls so near to us.

On January 18th our Hindustani brother started with the carts which carried all that we should need during our stay in Datia, and we joined him there the next day, having driven out in our own conveyance over the best of roads. We took up our abode in the Raja's rest-house provided for travellers, which is pleasantly situated about two miles from the city. The city is surrounded by a high wall, while within the city another wall equally high encloses the grounds belonging to the Raja's palace, and excludes from view the palace itself. Not a single European lives in Datia, and here the signs of civilisation could hardly be fewer, if in all India there were not one representative of the western world.

Since our first visit to this city, the railway has been completed which passes within sight of it. This railway is now the mail route from Bombay to the Funjab, but its influence seems to have been even less than that of the cart-road in awakening enterprise in this sixteenth century town. At the little railway station the fast trains make no stop, the one slow train each way being more than sufficient to pick up any travellers who prefer to pay the small cost of a quick and comfortable journey by rail rather than to go on foot. The macadamised road made by the British Government passes within less than two miles of the city, but travellers along this thoroughfare would not dream that so large a town lay so near at hand, were it not that two picturesque old palaces occupying prominent positions not far off cannot fail to arrest the attention of passers-by. As for signs of life outside the walls of the city of Datia, they are almost entirely wanting. To go from Datia to Gwalior on one side, or to Jhansi on the other, is like entering into a new world.

The preaching began in the town on the morning following our arrival, and a large crowd of people listened to the Gospel in one of the principal streets. After nightfall the preachers went again to the city, using the sciopticon and Bible pictures to attract an audience, and not without success. My husband having for some time been conducting two Sunday services in English for the Presbyterian soldiers of the garrison and other non-conformists at Jhansi, it was necessary for him to go home for the Sabbath. During his absence the Rev. Nabibakhsh continued to preach in the city, and seeing him alone, some of the people made bold to ask him by what authority he had come there to preach. "By the authority of the King of kings," was his answer, and he was allowed to proceed with his preaching undisturbed. No opposition whatever was encountered here, but no serious interest in the Gospel message was manifested by any one who listened to it. The spiritual darkness which enshrouds the masses of the people in any city in India, even the most progressive, is sufficiently depressing; in Datia it is a darkness which in a very exceptional degree makes itself felt.

An incident which occurred one evening will illustrate this. My husband had bought in the bazaar some grass for his pony, and before the bundles had been placed in his cart, a cow had snatched away one of them. Before she could devour it, however, it was rescued from her mouth; whereupon a Brahman, standing by, glared upon the Christians with angry eyes, and said in wrathful tones, "Would you take that grass from the mouth of God?"

From Datia flying visits were paid to Barauni, a large village among the hills, five or six miles off, and to Sonagir, about the same distance away. The latter village is a place of some note, on account of its Jain temples, which attract many pilgrims. These temples, some of which are fine specimens of architecture, crown a rocky ridge, and are seen from afar. The golden pinnacles of these temples may possibly have given to the place its name, which means "hill of gold." Before starting to Sonagir on his pony, my husband filled his pockets with booklets in Hindi, which were bought with avidity by the people about the temples, the last one having been sold before he left the place. In Datia, Barauni and Sonagir at least five hundred Gospel booklets must have been sold, as the amount realised from sales amounted to more than eight rupees.

On the day of our arrival in Datia my husband called on the *Díwán* (the Raja's chief official), and had an extended interview with him, during which he stated the object of his visit to the Raja's capital. This functionary was surrounded according to custom by a large number of attendants, all of whom had an opportunity of hearing the conversation which took place. The *Díwán* took occasion to tell my husband that he was a Brahman, and would much prefer to be engaged in his proper occupation as a priest, but that the office which he held had been thrust upon him. One of his attendants approached my husband for the purpose of putting a mark upon his forehead, which, however, he declined. The *Díwán* then explained that it was a mark of honor which it was proper that he should bear, because he was a religious teacher. He politely allowed him to decline it, however, as contrary to Christian custom.

During this call my husband remarked to the *Díwán* that he and his wife hoped to have the pleasure during their stay in Datia of seeing the various places of interest in and around the city. This was no sooner said than the *Díwán* offered to send one of the Raja's carriages to take us out sight-seeing that afternoon, if it would be our pleasure to go at that time. This offer was accepted with thanks, and at the appointed hour the carriage appeared at the rest-house, with a guide to accompany us in our round. Of all that we saw, that which interested us most was the old and long unused palace, built by the celebrated Bundela chief, Bir Singh Deo of Orcha. This stands outside the city, and commands a splendid prospect.

A novel spectacle which on more than one occasion amused us while we were in Datia was a company of boys in uniform, performing military evolutions under an instructor. On inquiring the meaning of this, I was told that the Raja, having no son to succeed him, had implored the gods to bestow such a gift upon him, and had vowed that should his request be granted, he would equip and maintain a troop of boy-soldiers. A son was given. There was great rejoicing, and the Raja, remembering his vow, and anxious to ensure the life of his heir, gave an order that a certain number of boys should be collected at his capital, and be fed, clothed and instructed in military tactics at his expense. Barracks had been provided for these juvenile soldiers, and they were in all respects well cared for.

Having devoted to Datia and its neighborhood all the time which we could spare, we returned to Jhansi, as we had planned to make a short tour in another direction.

February 1st, 1888, was a memorable day for us, as on this date the first of the lines of railway extending to Jhansi was opened for traffic. This was the branch of the Indian Midland System connecting Jhansi with Cawnpore. We had watched with the deepest interest the progress made in the construction of this iron road, which was destined to do so much in aid of missionary work, and it was for us a happy circumstance that our first use of it was to go forth to preach the Gospel of Christ. My husband bought the first tickets sold at the Jhansi railway station, and we took our seats in the first passenger train leaving this place.

We proceeded to Moth, a large town thirty-two miles distant from Jhansi, and there made our first encampment, our plan being to go to places nearer home after visiting some of the villages in this more remote part of our field. When on Saturday it was necessary for my husband to go home for the Sabbath, we had reason to be thankful for the railway which enabled him to make the journeys to and fro so quickly and comfortably. We remained a week in Moth, during which time the Gospel was preached there and in the surrounding villages.

Seven miles from Moth is Sumpthar, where a petty Raja bears sway. As we were so near this place, we determined to set up our tents there for a few days. On the way to Sumpthar, if we had been blindfolded, we could have told by most painful experience of the roughness of the road that we were no longer in British territory. On arriving at our destination we found nothing worthy to be called a town, but only an extensive conglomeration of low huts in an extremely dilapidated condition. The population of the village could hardly have exceeded three thousand, but there stood beside it, and in strangest contrast with it, a well preserved fort of huge dimensions. On this useless stronghold money was being freely expended, while everything outside of it seemed to be abandoned to decay. We visited a dispensary which had at some time been established in imitation of the English, and found it a dispensary only in name, the building having been so long neglected that the larger part of it was no longer habitable. A bungalow, once used as a guest-house for European visitors, was also in ruin. The streets were full of people in holiday attire, and when we asked what had brought together this multitude, we were told that a marriage was about to take place in the Raja's family, and that these crowds of people had, according to custom, come from the surrounding villages to enjoy the festivities, and to be fed. On the day of our arrival, and while our camp was being put in order, the Raja came to see us. After learning who we were, and the object of our visit, he said to my husband, "You must teach me also." These words sounded well, but they were intended to be only complimentary. We did not see the Raja again, but to his people in Sumpthar and in two neighboring villages the Gospel was preached.

Leaving Sumpthar we returned to the railway at Poonch, forty-one miles from Jhansi, and here our camp remained five days. It was a relief to exchange the idle throng at Sumpthar for the quiet work at Poonch. When Saturday came, my husband went again to Jhansi for the Sabbath. While we were at Poonch, the Rev. Patrick R. Mackay, pastor of the Free Church, Prestonpans, Scotland, who was spending the cold season in evangelistic work in India, wrote proposing to pay us a visit in Jhansi, in order to hold some meetings for the soldiers of the garrison. I accordingly returned home to entertain our guest, while my husband took advantage of his presence in Jhansi over the Sabbath, to visit some of the more distant towns of our district.

Turning eastward from Poonch, my husband's camp was pitched first at Irich, a Mahomedan town, where large and quiet audiences heard the Word; then at Gursarai, which is the head-quarters of a Mahratta chief, whose estate comprises sixty-three villages, situated in the heart of the British district of Jhansi; and from there he went on to Garotha, forty-five miles distant from Jhansi, this being the farthest point which he had planned to reach. On the way back he made two encampments in small villages, and the railway was reached again at Chirgaun, a large town twenty miles from our home, where a brief halt was made.

Not until a missionary in India begins to move about among the villages and towns of the district given him as his field of labor, can he have any adequate realisation of the work to be done in giving the Gospel to these myriads of people. To say nothing of the great number of inhabitants of the Datia, Sumpthar, Gursarai and Orcha territories at our very door, there were in the British district of Jhansi, according to the census of 1901, no less than 1,340 towns and villages, containing 616,759 inhabitants. Such are the dimensions of our one parish in Bundelkhand. Is it to be wondered at, that we are led to say, What are we, and our little band of Hindustani helpers, among so many? We are making a beginning, but when can the end of the work of evangelising these hundreds of thousands be reached, if others, yea, many others, are not sent to help us?

Jesus had at first twelve apostles to aid him in preaching the Gospel in the little land of Israel. Afterwards he appointed seventy others, and sent them two and two before his face into every city and place, whither he himself was about to come. That was a very large increase in the mission force. There was then a preaching band of eighty-two, headed by the Lord himself. And yet it was just after this great increase in the number of our Lord's chosen fellow-workers, that he said to his disciples, "The harvest indeed is plenteous, but the laborers are few: pray ye therefore the Lord of the harvest, that he send forth laborers into his harvest."

Are not the actions and words of Jesus concerning the work in which he himself was engaged as an itinerant missionary in the land of Israel, a sufficient comment upon the needs of the great mission field of the world at the beginning of this twentieth century of the Christian era?

The great need of the great harvest field of the world is laborers—laborers thrust forth by the Lord of the harvest into His own harvest field; for only those whom He Himself thrusts forth can reap His harvest. And what could be plainer than that the Lord desires that the need of laborers for His harvest field should be fully and speedily met, when He tells His people to look to Him to thrust them forth?

The Churches of India must eventually supply the numerous agents and agencies which will be required for the work of bringing the people of India to Christ; but at the present stage of the missionary enterprise in this land, there is the most urgent need of many more foreign missionaries to act as leaders and educators of those whom the Lord is now raising up, and will raise up, from among the people of the land, to build up His Church and Kingdom here.

XIV.

THE BOY NABIBAKHSH.

One summer afternoon about sixty years ago a boy named Nabibakhsh, seven or eight years of age, was playing with some companions in one of the streets of the city of Lucknow. A horseman passing leisurely along, reined in his steed, and with an interested eye watched the children at their play. When one of these had won a victory in the game, the stranger cried out, "*Shábásh!*" (bravo!). Then turning to the victor, little Nabibakhsh, he said, "Come here, my man, and I will lift you up beside me, and give you a ride."

This was a fine opportunity to mount a horse, and the boy without hesitancy allowed the man to lift him to the saddle, and place him before him. The man then gave his horse a prod, and the animal broke into a brisk canter. The youthful rider was elated, and his companions looked after him with envy. The speed did not slacken, and soon the riders were beyond the limits of the city. "Let me down now," said the boy, "or I shall not know the way back." "This I cannot do," replied the man; "we are already so far from Lucknow, that it would be impossible for you to find your way home, so I must take you with me." The boy began to cry, but was told that this would avail nothing, as he would not be allowed to go back. The child was much frightened, for he realised that he was entirely at the mercy of this stranger. Not until nightfall did the riders dismount. Lifting the boy, who was stiff and sore, from the saddle, his captor shoved him rudely into a hut; then telling him that some food would be sent to him, he closed the door. Bitter were the tears the boy shed when he was left alone. He thought of his mother, a widow, who would wait for his coming, and of his brother and sister who would miss their playmate. "Shall I ever see them again? and where, O! where, is this terrible man going to take me?" he asked himself again and again. After eating the food which was sent to him, he was soon overcome by weariness, and knew nothing until a little before day-break he was roughly shaken, and told to be ready for the journey which was to be resumed. Halting only a short time in the middle of the day for food, and again only when night overtook them, the travellers continued their journey until the city of Rampur was reached, distant one hundred and eighty-five miles from Lucknow. They were to go no further; and now began a reign of terror for the defenceless boy. His allowance of food was scanty, his tasks were heavy, and frequent blows were inflicted upon him by his tormentor, who seemed to take a savage delight in torturing his victim. He was so cruelly beaten that he bears the marks of his keeper's brutality to this day.

Wearily the months dragged on, and there seemed to be no hope of deliverance. At last the boy driven to desperation resolved to make an effort to escape. Closely guarded as he was, he knew that this would be wellnigh impossible, but his bondage had become intolerable. The thought of gaining his freedom was so sweet, that he was helped thereby to bear with some degree of resignation his bitter lot, in the hope that a door of escape would soon open to him. His master, taking the boy's seeming indifference to blows as an indication that he had found it wise to submit to his fate, watched him less closely than formerly. When at length the cruel master was obliged to be absent from home for an entire day, he left heavy tasks for his slave to perform during his absence.

Now, the lad felt, was his opportunity; and no sooner was his tormentor far enough away to make it safe for him to attempt his escape, than he took to his heels. He had by this time become sufficiently acquainted with the neighborhood of his abode to enable him to choose unfrequented paths, and thus escape observation. On he sped like a frightened deer, unmindful of fatigue, heat, hunger or thirst. When night overtook him he was far distant from Rampur. By the way he had begged enough food to satisfy his hunger, and he laid himself down and slept soundly.

With the first streak of dawn he was again on his way, and each mile which separated him from his persecutor put new courage into his heart, though he was tired and footsore, and knew not what was before him. His one desire and uppermost thought was to make sure of his escape from bondage. He continued his flight until he reached the city of Bareilly, thirty-nine miles from Rampur. He was unable to go further. Found by a policeman, he was taken to the English magistrate, a man full of kindness, who was touched by the sad condition of the homeless waif. The marks of the scourgings he had received bore witness to the truth of his story. The magistrate comforted the boy, and took him to his own house, where he was well fed, and good clothes were provided for him. To receive such treatment made him feel that he was in a new world.

As it was found impossible to obtain any trace of the

child's relatives, the magistrate resolved to send him to the American Presbyterian Orphanage in Fatehgarh, where the missionaries, the Rev. J. L. Scott and his wife, would take good care of him, and where also he would be educated and trained for usefulness. When the magistrate made known to the little fellow his intentions concerning him, he was very happy. Truly his condition had undergone a great change, when such kind words were spoken to him, and his wellbeing had become matter for such consideration.

The hunted look which his face had worn now gave place to that quiet and trustful expression which is the heritage of childhood. When arrangements had been completed for his journey to Fatehgarh, seventy-five miles distant, he was dressed in clean clothes, and seating himself in the *doolee* (swing-litter) which had been provided for his conveyance, was borne away. According to written instructions which accompanied him, his safety and comfort were at each stage of the way to be carefully looked after, and he was to be sent forward to his destination without delay.

In due time he arrived safely at the mission house in Fatehgarh and presented a letter from the magistrate at Bareilly, delivering him into the care of the mission, and relating all that was known of his history. Remaining in the orphanage a number of years, Nabibakhsh, by his ready obedience, diligence in study and trustworthiness, grew in the esteem of the missionaries, and was beloved by his associates. He united with the Church on the profession of his faith in Christ as his Saviour, and when fitted for the work of a preacher, was made a catechist. At length when Etawah was made a station of the mission, and the Rev. J. F. Ullmann was sent to begin the work there, Nabibakhsh accompanied him to that station as a helper; and there under the careful tuition of this missionary he was prepared for the ministry. He was then ordained by the Presbytery of Furrukhabad, and installed as pastor of the Hindustani Church in Etawah.

While living in Etawah pastor Nabibakhsh met with a sudden and terrible bereavement. During an exceptionally heavy storm of rain his house collapsed, burying in its ruins his wife and little ones. His three children were killed, and his wife was injured, but not fatally.

It was in Etawah that our first six months in India were spent. During this period the Rev. J. F. Ullmann was our tutor in Hindustani, and there we made the acquaintance of pastor Nabibakhsh, who sixteen years later came to help us in our work in Jhansi. God has made his bow to abide in strength, for he is still with us, and continues to preach the Gospel with great acceptance.

XV.

FIRST FINANCIAL HELP FOR THE WORK.

When it was decided that Jhansi should be occupied conditionally, it was with the explicit understanding that until the financial prospects in America brightened, or at least until formal sanction for the permanent occupation of this new field should be given by the Board in New York, no extra expense beyond the rent of the bungalow should be incurred. The gifts which came to us at this time were therefore especially opportune.

For nearly two years before we left Allahabad, a number of young ladies had met once a month at our bungalow for the purpose of gaining a knowledge of missionary work in different parts of the world. The majority of them belonged to the congregation of the Scotch Kirk, and several of them had been my pupils in the Sunday-school connected with this Church. We studied India as a mission field, and also Africa. As their knowledge of missions increased, in a like ratio increased the interest of the members of this circle in the spiritual welfare of the unevangelised in their own and in other lands. The first money contributed by them was applied toward the support of one of the orphan girls in our own charge at Allahabad. And the first contribution which we received in our new field in aid of our work, was made by the young ladies of this mission band. This unexpected gift moved me deeply, and the gratitude which the givers expressed for the effort I had made to lead them out of themselves, and to teach them to have a care for others, touched me more tenderly still.

Some time during our first summer in Jhansi, the foreign mail brought us a letter written in an unfamiliar hand. On opening it we found that it contained a draft for five pounds sterling. The letter and the gift came from a lady in America whom we had known before coming to India, but of whom we had heard nothing for many years. We had been much on her heart of late, she wrote, and she had been moved to send a small gift to aid us in our work. The lady knew nothing of our transfer from Allahabad to Jhansi, or of our special needs; but the Lord knew, and he had put it into her heart to send us this money at this particular time. Two other letters received about the same time brought each a contribution for our work.

During our last year in Allahabad the pastor of one of our Presbyterian Churches in America, while travelling through India on his way to Australia, gave us a passing call. His sojourn in Australia for physical recuperation led to his becoming the pastor of the Cairns Memorial Presbyterian Church in Melbourne. He was not forgotten after he went from us, but to him, as well as to many others whom we sought to interest in our new field, a letter was sent. The Melbourne pastor, after perusing this letter, handed it to an "elect lady" of his Church, knowing that she would be interested in its contents. This handmaid of the Lord, who was full of zeal for the Master's work abroad as well as at home, read with peculiar pleasure this communication from a stranger in India, because, as she afterwards wrote, it furnished the information which she and other ladies of her Church had long desired to obtain. They had wished to aid in work among the women of India in some needy field, but knew not how or where they could do this. My letter to their pastor furnished the necessary link, wrote this lady in the first communication which she sent to me. A great interest in our work, she further said, had been awakened among the ladies of the Cairns Memorial Church by the letter which I had written to their pastor, and as a thank-offering for the information they had received, a contribution of ten pounds sterling was sent to help in building our church. "We rejoice," she wrote, "that we are allowed the privilege of adding a few bricks to your church, and we pray that within its walls souls may be born for the Church above."

In my letter I had made mention of meeting many of the Jhansi women at the Five Wells, and had said that by this means I had obtained an entrance to some of their homes. Our newly-found friends desired to aid me in the work I was trying to do in these homes, and my correspondent said, "Tell me in what way we can help you in your work among the women." In reply I said that we greatly needed an experienced zenana teacher, and mentioned the sum which I thought would be required to pay the salary of such a teacher. A prompt response came, pledging the sum of sixty pounds sterling annually for this purpose, and authorising me to secure as soon as possible the services of a suitable person. This was accordingly done, and the yearly contribution promised by the Melbourne ladies was continued for five years. At the expiration of this period, the help from Australia ceased, only because the Australian Churches had then begun to send missionaries of their own to India. Our Melbourne friends had helped us when help from them was most welcome, and when they could no longer continue to aid us, on account of demands made upon them to support work in India carried on by missionaries sent from Australia, our own Church in America was in a position to take up the burden which they laid down.

Other generous gifts for our work afterwards reached us, but they are not mentioned in this connection, as the object of this chapter is to speak only of the financial help which we received at the time of our greatest need.

XVI.

INTEREST FELT IN THIS FIELD.

We can never cease to be grateful for the deep interest manifested, from the beginning, in the work in Jhansi, by the ladies of the Philadelphia Board. Realising as they seemed to do in a remarkable degree what wide doors of usefulness God had opened for us here, and as a consequence of this, how many and pressing were our needs, they lent willing hands in laying the foundations which the work in its infancy required. They promptly assumed the responsibility of providing means for the purchase of the house which had been rented for our use, and so zealous and successful were their efforts to this end, that not long after the Board in New York had given its formal sanction to the permanent occupation of Jhansi as a mission station, the money needed to secure the property had all been obtained.

It was a great gratification to us that Dr. John C. Lowrie, the Senior Secretary of our Board, who had been the first missionary sent to India by our Church, felt a special interest in the opening of this part of India to the Gospel. After a meeting of the Board in New York in April, 1887, Dr. Lowrie wrote that it had been decided to defer the main question, that is, in reference to the permanent occupation of Jhansi, for some months; but he added for our encouragement these

OUR HOUSE IN JHANSI.

words, "The feeling here is, I think, favorable to our occupying this post. To me, personally, it is of some interest that Bundelkhand, in which Jhansi is situated, was one of the fields under consideration, when the north-western field was chosen in 1834."

To one who knew how earnestly we desired to remain in Jhansi, and who hoped that our desire might be fulfilled, Dr. Lowrie wrote two months later, "I sympathise with Mr. and Mrs. Holcomb about Jhansi, and I trust that their warm expectations may be fulfilled." In the same letter he referred to the depressed business condition of the country, and the state of the Board's treasury which necessitated a reduction of eight and a half per cent. on the estimates for all the stations of the mission. A discouraging prospect, truly, when the taking up of a new field was under consideration.

In September Dr. Lowrie, writing to the mission, spoke of the gloomy financial outlook in America, and in reference to this, said, "You can easily understand, dear brethren, that the state of things here makes it the duty of the Board to go on, if at all, with extreme caution." Then referring once more to Jhansi, he added, "Well, if it be the Lord's will that Jhansi should become one of our stations, then, in due time, all will be made plain; and peradventure the conferences and prayer of 1834, when Bundelkhand and the Protected Sikh States were in the scales, may be happily settled by the occupation of both in the general work of our Church in India. If it be the Lord's will, may it be so ordered."

At length, when it was decided by the Board that Jhansi should be permanently occupied, and the money for the purchase of the house in which we were living, had been provided by the ladies of the Woman's Foreign Missionary Society of Philadelphia, Dr. Lowrie when acknowledging this generous and timely assistance, said in his letter to the treasurer of this Society, "I think it was a decided advance in our work to have secured as a station the chief city of Bundelkhand, and I feel grateful to you all for your good gifts for the purchase of the property in Jhansi.

Toward the close of the summer of 1888 an Anglo-Indian gentleman came from Agra to Jhansi to reside. He had passed through the scenes of the Mutiny, and had just published a pamphlet in which he had given an account of his experiences during that trying time. From Jhansi he sent a copy of this pamphlet to a retired military officer, Major Conran, of Ixworth, England, whom he had known in India. When acknowledging the receipt of the pamphlet, Major Conran asked his friend, "Is there any missionary work in Jhansi?" and then added, "I have thought much about getting the Gospel there since our campaigns in 1840-42."

During his service in India this military officer had found Christ, or rather the Good Shepherd had found his lost sheep, and from the time when he became a Christian he had consecrated all that he was, and all that he had, to the service of his Lord and Master. His letter to his friend in Jhansi was placed in my hands that I might reply to his inquiry about the missionary work; and knowing that he would be interested in learning about the work which we had begun in Jhansi, I wrote to him fully concerning the changed condition in Bundelkhand, and in Jhansi in particular, relating the circumstances connected with our coming to this new field, and telling him of the work begun by us, and of the opportunities for doing good which were open to us on every hand. This communication drew forth from him a most sympathetic reply, a part of which is here quoted.

"IXWORTH, SUFFOLK, ENGLAND.

DEAR MRS. HOLCOMB—You cannot imagine the delight with which I received your letter. It came like a dream over my spirit, recalling the times that were past, when I used by faith to expect that Christ's Kingdom would surely be established in Bundelkhand. You have only to read my autobiography to understand it. My faith could not be said to have become quenched in the many years that have since elapsed without a word of tidings regarding accomplishment.

Writing to my father, who had been there in 1786, of my hope to carry the Gospel into Central India, when appointed as adjutant there in 1840, I recollect how I portrayed the misery of the millions still sitting in darkness; and now I could hardly believe my eyes when I looked on the map and saw railroads and mission stations throughout the province. Thinking of the providential dealings which have brought some of these changes about, I am like old Jacob when he exclaimed, "Joseph is yet alive!" and as if to add the climax, I've just heard of my old regiment (so I call it, having been among the men so often to distribute tracts when they were at home) as stationed at Jhansi. May you be helped to win many souls amongst them.

'All these things are against me,' I used to say when all my schemes for schools and native preachers were frustrated by a sudden call to fresh campaigning. What unbelievers we are at the best! Because all my old mission friends and the pillars of the Church were removed, I used to say, 'Wheeler is not, and Duff is not, and they will take away Lawrence and Edwardes also;' but I see that instead of the fathers we have the children, the Janviers, the Newtons, the Morrisons; and better still, we have the Lord, "the same yesterday and to-day and forever." The Government is upon his shoulders. He is the Wonderful Counsellor.

Here I must explain for fear you should expect too much from me, that I, being much interested in the work of your Board, some fifty years ago made over to them a sum of money to establish a mission for Afghanistan, the country then most neglected, and the late Mr. Loewenthal was accordingly sent to Peshawar for the purpose, and labored around those wild tracts, the Black Mountains, and other places amongst the Afghans, until through an accident he was shot, having been taken for a robber, when he was walking about his compound at night. But he had finished his work, had given to the Afghans a translation of the New Testament in Pushtoo. He was a man of great erudition.

But to the point. I had put aside a sum of money for this my pet project, and had corresponded with Dr. Lowrie, urging that Mr. Loewenthal's place be filled; but after many appeals, I found my strength failing, and as I knew not the day of my death, I felt the responsibility of keeping the Lord's money idle, perhaps to fall into unworthy hands; so two or three years ago, after inviting other Societies in vain to engage in it (the work which Mr. Loewenthal had laid down), I made over the money put aside for the Afghan mission, to the Salvation Army, impressed with the zeal they manifested toward all lands. What a pity I had not known of the Bundelkhand enterprise! However, money is a poor means of effecting God's purposes. When I think of the thousands of noble lives that have been spent on behalf of India's salvation, of the men, women and children of whom the world was not worthy, who have died at their posts, not having seen the promises, why! in their bodies buried beneath the soil of India, some of them under the snows of Cabul, they have already taken possession of the land, and of those everlasting hills; for Christ. God does not require our money. The Kingdom is the Lord's, and He is the Ruler over the nations.

I shall anticipate further news with deepest interest. My time is short, and if I can do anything toward forwarding the Gospel in Central India, it will lighten my journey and hurry me home. The Lord bless you and yours.

Believe me, dear friends,
Affectionately yours,
H. CONRAN."

It was through Major Conran that Mrs. Kemp of Brighton, England, mentioned in a previous chapter, heard of our work in Jhansi. Major Conran and Dr. Kemp had worked together for Christ in Peshawar; and subsequently the work which Dr. Kemp had done in Jhansi had served to revive the interest which Major Conran had sixteen years before begun to feel in Bundelkhand. When Major Conran received the news that our mission had entered upon work in Jhansi, it delighted him to communicate the same to his old Indian friend, Mrs. Kemp, and thus through an interesting chain of circumstances was much prayer, of that kind which we cannot but believe availeth much in its working, enlisted on our behalf.

Major Conran continued to feel a very deep interest in our work in Jhansi, sending us from time to time letters full of good cheer, and to aid in the erection of our church edifice we received from him a substantial gift of money. On our return from furlough to America in the autumn of 1893, we enjoyed the privilege of spending a few hours with this saint of God in his home in Ixworth. Sitting by his fireside he passed away on the 23rd of February, 1902, praying over and over again, "May the glory of the Lord cover the whole earth." "He had no thought except to do good," wrote the lady in whose family he had lived since 1876. He had been his own executor, and the means which he possessed had been used for the spread of the Gospel in his lifetime.

XVII.

A ZENANA TEACHER SECURED, AND A SCHOOL FOR GIRLS ESTABLISHED.

The funds needed for the support of an experienced and efficient zenana teacher having been obtained, we set about to secure a suitable person for this work. Mrs. Seymour, whose services were engaged, and who began her work in Jhansi in July 1888, had spent ten years as a zenana teacher in the cities of Allahabad and Agra.

We intended to establish a school for girls as soon as we could do so, there being as much need for this as for zenana teaching. And for this work, as well as for the teaching of the women in their homes, there was an open door. Among the clerks employed in the railway offices were many Bengalis, and others who like the Bengalis had in other places where they had lived known more or less of the advantages enjoyed in mission schools, and they desired that not only the women of their households, but their girls also should become our pupils. Said a Bengali gentleman one day to my husband, "We are anxious to have a school established for our daughters." And a Hindustani gentleman who called upon us one evening said, "Our wives and daughters are very ignorant, but no one here has ever taken an interest in them. In other places schools have been established for girls, and the women are taught in their homes." We were glad that we could say to these persons, that what missionaries were doing in other places, we intended to do in Jhansi.

Sooner than we had expected, we were able to start a school for girls; for when Mrs. Seymour came to us, she brought with her a daughter who had had some experience as a teacher, and was fitted to take the position of headmistress of such a school.

The school was opened about the middle of July in a small bungalow in the mission compound. We determined to establish this school on our own premises outside the city, rather than in the city itself, because here it could be more satisfactorily supervised, and also because it would be well for the pupils to be removed on school days from the pernicious influences inseparable from life amidst heathenish surroundings. The change to the different scenes and influences of the mission compound would, we felt, be in itself no unimportant element in the education of the children. We anticipated that many of the parents, if not all of them, would object to letting their children come to a school outside the city, and so it was no more than we expected when Mrs. Seymour encountered considerable opposition as in her rounds of teaching in the houses she sought to secure pupils for this school. "How can I send my children so far away from me? And how can I allow them to be absent so long? Who knows what may befall them outside the city?" said more than one anxious mother.

In one house where a mother was urging her objections, the father sitting by asked, "Under whose control will this school be?" "It will be under the control of a missionary lady," was answered. "Then my daughters may go," was the prompt response of the father; and he added, "When I was a lad, I attended a school in Saharanpur, which was superintended by the Rev. Mr. Caldwell, an American missionary, and I know that in a mission school my children will be safe, and will get only good." Thus two bright little girls were secured for the school.

In other houses objections were in various ways overcome, and we soon had a goodly number of very interesting pupils, the majority of them belonging to high-caste and well-to-do families. We had felt that if such pupils could be secured for the school at the beginning, it would be easier to induce those who were lower in the social scale to commit their children to our care. The people of Jhansi, of all classes, had yet to learn the value of the privileges which mission schools afford, and so when they saw that their Bengali and Hindustani neighbors unhesitatingly entrusted their children to us, a good object lesson was set before them.

The children soon became very fond of the school, and they greatly enjoyed their rides to and fro in the mission carts. One little child, on the first day of her appearance in the school, as she looked with delighted eyes upon the company of happy children gathered together, exclaimed, "It's just like a mela" (a Hindu festival), which expressed her highest idea of happiness.

When the school was first opened the children were unwilling to enter the bungalow in which we lived. "Perhaps we might in this way be made Christians," they said. One little girl, whose father was somewhat advanced in his ideas, said, "I am not afraid to go, and my father will not object"; so daily she came for books, pencils or whatever was required in the school.

After a time others ventured into our house, and it was not long until it was regarded as a great privilege to come to our bungalow.

The girls proved themselves to be not one whit behind their brothers in trying to drive a hard bargain, and some time passed before they became convinced that we transacted business in an entirely straightforward way, adhering strictly to the "one price" system. An incident which one day occurred will illustrate not only the shrewdness, but the duplicity which these juveniles sometimes exhibited. A little girl coming into the room where I was accustomed to receive the children, saw on my table a new pair of small scissors. "Are these for sale?" she inquired. 'You may have them, if you wish,' I answered, and the price was named. "May I take them home to show to my mother?" was the next question asked. Permission to take them to her home was given, but the child was told that if she brought back the scissors, they must be returned in as good condition as they were in when taken from the bungalow. On the following morning the little maiden appeared, and holding out towards me in her slender palm a coin whose value was one-third less than the price of the scissors, said, "My mother likes the scissors, but she thinks the price too high." And then touching with one of her fingers the coin in her open palm, she added, "She is willing to give this." 'Very well,' I said, 'put the scissors on the table; I have but one price.' "And you will not take this?" she inquired. 'Certainly not,' I answered firmly. Whereupon, holding out her right arm, and placing under the extended sleeve her left hand, she let drop into it another coin, which made up what was lacking in the price I had named. Then quite unabashed she laid the two bits of silver on the table, took up the scissors, made a graceful salaam, and tripped out of the room.

I have said that the children became very fond of the school. To such an extent was this the case, that neither the fierce heat of the summer, nor the heavy rain of the monsoon kept them at home. During April and until the summer vacation began some time in May, the school opened at half-past six in the morning, and closed at eleven o'clock. On one of the hottest days at this season of the year the woman who collected the children came in haste from the school-room to our bungalow to tell me that one of the girls had swooned, and was lying in an unconscious state on one of the benches. I went over at once and found one of the brightest and best-beloved children in the school lying pale and limp on one of the forms, and with beads of cold perspiration on her brow. As she was from a high-caste family, I was afraid to administer any thing for her relief, lest the cry should be raised that I had interfered with her caste. 'What can have caused this?' I asked, as I stood by her side. "I think she is weak because she hurried away from home without taking any food, lest she should be late at school, and she has been overcome by the heat," said her younger sister in reply. The child was very delicate, and her weakness seemed to be the only cause of her fainting. Presently she opened her eyes, and wished to sit up. Just at this juncture I heard a fruit-vendor crying out, "Oranges, sweet oranges." 'Just what I want,' I thought; and I went out and bought some of them. I then handed one to the woman who attended upon the children, telling her to remove the loose skin, and feed the pulp to the child. This was just what she needed, as it supplied the necessary food and drink. When she was sufficiently revived and strengthened, I sent her home in a closed conveyance, and thus ended my anxiety for the little one who had denied herself food that morning that she might not be late at the school.

Some of the children in the school made surprising progress, notably two Bengali girls, who had been learning not only Bengali, but Hindi and English. On one occasion when the schoolmistress was absent through illness, I asked these two girls to take the Bengali classes. Though but nine or ten years of age, they did not hesitate, but came forward promptly and began to teach with all the dignity of young ladyhood. There was nothing in their demeanor to indicate that they were "playing teacher." After having first heard each the recitations of the other, they divided the classes between them, and proceeded with the lessons. They prepared copies for those pupils who were learning to write Bengali, and looked over the examples of those who were studying arithmetic, checking off those which were correctly done, exactly as they had seen their teacher do.

The girls are very fond of singing, and the Christian songs which they learn in the school are often heard in their homes. Because of this, one very promising pupil was removed from the school. "She is singing your songs from morning until night," the mother had said to the zenana teacher. And then she added, "I do not mind this myself, but her uncle is displeased, and insists that she must be removed from such influences."

It was a grievous disappointment to us when as time passed on, some of the older children, though they were still very young, were withdrawn from the school in order that they might be married. The mother of one of these child-wives once remarked to Mrs. Seymour

"When my little girl was in school, she was always well; now she is always ill."

Some of the girls after they are married are still taught by us in their homes, but others after they leave the school are never seen by us again.

Very young girls are sometimes removed from the school simply because they are considered too old to be seen outside their homes; and they are sometimes detained at home when their own parents would gladly allow them to continue in the school. "Why do your girls not come now to the school?" a mother was one day asked, as she sat before the zenana teacher, book in hand. "*She* will not let them go," she answered in a low voice, pointing at the same time to a room where the grandmother of our former pupils, wrinkled and toothless and with hair of snowy whiteness, was bustling noisily about. She had recently taken up her abode in this house, and her advent was the cause of the removal of the girls from the school. "Only get *her* consent," continued the mother, "and we will gladly send the children to the school again." The old woman, though apparently very busily occupied at the time, overheard this conversation, and with flashing eyes soon confronted Mrs. Seymour and her pupil. "Send these girls to school!" she scornfully exclaimed. "Look at them! they are too old to go to school." The girls to whom our attention was thus directed were only seven or eight years of age.

When about to leave India for a visit to England, the wife of the magistrate of our district, who had taken a deep interest in our compound school, asked what she could do during her absence to help us in our work. 'If you could send some gifts for the holiday-treat of the children in the school, it would help us much,' I answered.

"I shall be delighted to do so," was the prompt reply. And so before the next holiday-season came round, a large box containing a generous supply of toys and other useful gifts for the pupils, and suitable presents for the teachers, was received from our good friend. The supply of various articles was so ample, and there was so great a variety in the gifts, that we resolved to have something which would be entirely new to the children—a Christmas-tree. So when the time came, a large tent was pitched in the compound, and the best substitute for a fir-tree which could be procured was firmly planted in the middle of the tent. One of our very kind friends, the wife of the English commissioner, furnished the ornaments and the wax tapers, and several friends assisted in fastening these, together with the presents, upon the branches of the tree. When the exercises held in the school-room, consisting of singing, recitations, etc., were concluded, the children in orderly form marched out, and were admitted one by one to the darkened tent, in which stood the illuminated tree, which was loaded with the beautiful things that were to be distributed among them. When all were inside the tent, and the curtain at the entrance had been closed, absolute silence reigned for a moment. Then followed a murmur of suppressed delight, characteristic of Indian children; and the distribution of gifts began. When the tree had been denuded of its treasures, the little people who had watched the operation with the deepest interest, filed slowly out of the tent, each one making a graceful salaam. Carefully protecting the gifts they had received, they took their places in the school carts, and returned to their homes. The day was one which they could never forget, and from it dated an attachment for the school much greater than they had ever before felt.

THE GIRLS' SCHOOL.

XVIII.

MRS. SEYMOUR'S WORK IN THE ZENANAS.

The experiences of the zenana teacher are kaleidoscopic, but chiefly in the sense that they are endlessly varied. The teacher is ever and anon encouraged and stimulated in her work by the keenness of intellect with which the truth is perceived, and the apparent openness of heart with which it is accepted; but alternating with the brightness and receptiveness exhibited by certain pupils, are the apathy and dulness shown by others, with their accompanying effect upon the teacher of discouragement and depression: so that this work, though not unaccompanied by interesting incidents, requires, if not more than most kinds of missionary effort, most certainly not less than any other, unfailing patience and indefatigable zeal, in order to its being effectively prosecuted. Hence the necessity of securing for this work the services of such teachers as are physically, intellectually and spiritually qualified for engaging in it.

The work done by the zenana visitor is in great part that of teaching the women to read; but in every house visited, religious instruction is invariably given, and members of a household who are not learning to read, as well as women from adjoining houses, often gather around the teacher while the Gospel story is being told.

One day Mrs. Seymour found in a house which she was accustomed to visit, a number of strangers from a neighboring city. One or two *bhajans* were explained and sung, and then in simple language the way of salvation was set forth. "Tell us more, tell us more," cried one and another of the women. We are soon going back to our own city, and we may never have another opportunity of hearing these things."

Among our pupils was an interesting Bengali woman, the younger of whose two daughters came to our school. Very patient and gentle was this little mother. Her face was always sad and wistful, and she seemed to feel that there was a message for her in the truth which she heard. She always manifested much interest in the Bible lesson. Her little daughter was often absent from school on account of illness, and the mother told us that when suffering she said, "If I pray to Jesus, he will make me well." She found much comfort in repeating the hymns she had learned in the school.

Living near to this house was a family from the Punjab, in which we had pupils. There were seven women in this household, and with a single exception, all wore beautiful gold and silver ornaments. The eldest member of the family, a widow, was unadorned, but was well clothed. Two only were learning to read, but the others sat in the room while the Bible lesson was being given, and occasionally raised objections or suggested difficulties. One of the number, as she listened, deftly plied her needle. The little children of the household flitted in and out, the jewels which they wore making a musical sound as they ran about. A pretty boy, two years old, attracted by the singing, listened with eyes wide-open, and kept time with his bare feet, the silver bells on his tiny ankles tinkling softly with every motion. A pleasant house to visit was this one, but the minds of those who lived there were so occupied with the pleasures of this world that they had little if any thought for any thing beyond.

In a house where the mother, an intelligent and interesting woman, was receiving instruction, we one day found her three little daughters, who are pupils in our school, at home. After the reading-lesson was over, and a lesson from the Bible had also been given, the teacher, opening her book of *bhajans*, said, "What shall we sing?" Instantly the three little girls came forward, and the youngest promptly named her favorite. It was a beautiful sight—this loving, sweet-faced mother, surrounded by her pretty daughters, and all joining together in singing a Christian song, in their own language set to a native air.

In one of the zenanas a woman one day said to Mrs. Seymour, "We like your religion, and we admire your customs; we would gladly abandon the religion in which we have been reared, and become Christians; but how can we stand alone? We are but poor, weak women, and feel that we could not endure the separation from our families, and all the consequences which would surely follow the declaration of our change of faith."

Another woman said, when her relatives remonstrated with her for receiving instruction from a Christian teacher, "I shall continue to receive Christian teaching, for all the good I get comes from it. My caste people do nothing for me."

What it costs a woman from a heathen household in India to acknowledge herself a Christian, and receive Christian baptism, we can hardly estimate. In a majority of cases it costs her all of earth that she holds dear, the loss of her home, her husband, her children, her friends; and her name is by all her caste connections cast out as evil. The loss she sustains by becoming a

12

Christian is indeed great; and though her gain is infinite, yet this is a fact which she comes to understand only when the Great Teacher reveals it to her.

A relative of some of our pupils on coming from a neighboring city to visit his friends in Jhansi, was greatly annoyed when he found that in their house Christian instruction was being received. "The object of the Christian teacher is to make Christians of you," asserted the visitor. When one of the women said in reply, "I have not heard of any who have become Christians through this teaching," her friend added, "No matter whether or not any openly declare their change of views, they are being wrongly influenced, and the foundations of our ancestral faith are being destroyed. The seeds of error are being sown, and the fruit is sure to appear."

Occasionally a door is without any apparent reason closed against us. At the threshold of a house where Mrs. Seymour had been teaching she was one day met with the question, put in a very gruff manner, "Why do you come here?" "I have a pupil in this house," she answered; and she was permitted to enter, though the grim looks of the old man who had accosted her boded no good. Mrs. Seymour did not see her pupil. "We do not know where she is," said the other women of this house, who on former occasions had been most cordial in their behaviour, but who now seemed frightened, and anxious to be relieved of the presence of the visitor.

It is a wonder that Christian teachers are allowed to enter the zenanas at all. The fact that an entrance into their homes is obtained in spite of all difficulties and hindrances, and that we have so many invitations to come and teach, shows that the work is God's. The teachers of a false religion could never have such success. When one door is closed, another is opened; and the Christian teachers have all that they can do. It may be more or less difficult to make a beginning in a new place, as it was difficult for the pioneers in this work in India to inaugurate it, because its character was not understood, but a beginning having been made, the work progresses, and its progress is impeded only by the lack of means to carry it forward. However many may be the adversaries (and these are never wanting), there still remains the widely-open door.

When on one of her rounds Mrs. Seymour was leaving a house in which the elder members of the family had expressed a dislike to the Christian instruction given, a young man belonging to the household followed her, and as soon as he was beyond observation drew from his pocket a Bible, and holding it forth, said, "This book was given to me by a missionary. I was educated in a mission school, and I am truly grateful for all the Christian teaching I received while in that school, and I will do all I can to help you in getting pupils in the zenanas." To the question, "Do you read this book?" the young man replied, "I do."

One of our pupils who applied herself very diligently to her lessons, learned to read and write in a surprisingly short space of time. "I must learn all I can while I am here," said this energetic little woman, "for in a short time I shall go to a new home, and perhaps I shall not find there any one who can teach me." We put into this woman's hands when she was leaving us, some Christian tracts and the Gospels. Some time after her arrival at her new home she sent us, written in Hindi, in her own hand, a communication which did credit both to her mind and her heart.

But while occasionally a pupil is thus eager to learn, and makes astonishing progress, with the majority of those whom we teach, learning is a slow process, and the patience of the teacher is sorely tried. One woman of high-caste, the mother of a pupil in our girls' school, was so hopelessly dull that we should have been inclined to abandon the task of trying to teach her, had it not been evident that she was anxious to learn, and had not the visits to her house furnished a good opportunity for giving religious instruction to others as well as to her. The husband of this woman, a government servant, was after a time transferred to another station, and when Mrs. Seymour made her last visit to this house, her pupil threw herself at her feet and began to sob piteously. For a few moments she was unable to control her emotion; but presently she said, "I have been a dull pupil, I know; and how I have tried you! I have seen it in your face. But I am thankful that you did not give me up. I really did my best, and your visits have given me the brightest hour in all the week." We gave her tracts and Gospels to take with her to her new home. When after a few months she returned to Jhansi, she told us that among the acquaintances they had made in their new station, she had found a lad who could read well, and that he had read these books aloud to attentive and admiring audiences. Her neighbors there had begged her to leave these books with them when she was about to return to Jhansi. "I left the tracts," said the woman, "but I would not part with the Gospels."

A young woman whom Mrs. Seymour was asked to teach, began well, but soon grew weary of the task. "I do not care to learn," she said; "it is too difficult."

Then an elderly woman sitting by, said, "Why do

you so soon give up? I believe I could learn." "Try it then," was the answer. The woman took the discarded books into her wrinkled hands, held the open pages first near her eyes, then at a greater distance, and finally with a sigh closed the book, and said, "I really cannot see well enough to learn." After a little pause she added in a more cheerful tone, "But I can get spectacles, and then I can learn." This she did, and became a most interesting pupil, industrious and painstaking. She soon learned to read, and thus showed to the younger women in the house what could be done. Her countenance was pleasant to look upon, a smile lighting up her withered face as she wiped her glasses carefully and then adjusted them to her eyes in preparation for her lessons. In about a year this aged pupil was reading with ease the Gospel by John, and this was no less a satisfaction to us than to her.

Very different from this was the spirit manifested by another elderly woman whose granddaughter was one of our pupils. That this girl had remained so long unmarried had been cause for bitter complaint among the women of the household. To the grandmother especially it had been a great and constant grief. Though at last, arrangements had been made for her marriage, the old woman continued to grumble, saying, "She ought to have been married long ago, but her father got some new ideas into his head, and would not consent to it. He thinks girls should not be married so young." One morning when we visited this house the teaching went on without interruption until the Scripture lesson was taken up. Then the grandmother, who was sitting in a corner, broke forth into a tempest of wrath. "What you are reading is not true," said she; "I know all that you are accustomed to say," she added; "have I not heard it for years in Agra and other cities? I will not believe it. I shall cling to my own faith. That is the best for me. I hear about your religion constantly, for the Babu is forever reading to us out of your Book. I know it all, and I will not believe it." Sad it was to hear this aged pilgrim thus denouncing the truth. But how glad we were to learn that in this house was one who not only read the Bible, but read it to his household, even though his old mother scoffed at it!

There is much in the lives of those whose homes we visit which not only awakens in us a lively interest, but calls forth both our sympathy and our indignation.

The Hindu mother clasps her child to her breast with a love as true and fervent as that which pervades the heart of the more civilised mother in the western world, and when death claims her treasure, a void is left which cannot easily be filled. Here too we witness just such passions as mar the happiness of many homes in Christian lands—envy, jealousy, selfishness, and that fondness for the exercise of authority which takes little account of the rights of others.

On one occasion in a house where two young women, one of whom was bright and the other dull, had been learning to read, only the dull one appeared for her lesson. The other, who was very fond of her books, was engaged in some household occupation, and nodded to us as we passed, but when we called her to join us in the room where we were usually received, she was not allowed to come. Her aptitude and delight in learning had aroused the jealousy of the dull pupil, who unfortunately having authority in the household had spitefully forbidden her to read, and had imposed upon her such duties as left her no time for her loved lessons.

As might be expected, spoiled children are by no

means rare in Indian zenanas. In one house which we visited was a daughter who possessed unusual personal attractions. One day the mother said, "I have so much to do now, that I am always weary. My daughter who might help me is disinclined to do so. She will soon go to Calcutta to the house of her mother-in-law, and now her father when appealed to says, "Let her have a happy time while she can have it. She will soon have trouble enough." So the spoiled beauty was as undutiful toward her long-suffering mother, as is many a tenderly nurtured and much indulged daughter in more favored lands.

In Indian zenanas the mother-in-law is ever in evidence. Taking a seat one day on a low bed, which for our use had been drawn under the shade of a great *pipal* tree in a large, cool court-yard, we found the mother of the household in great trouble. She was folding, with many sighs, articles of gay, rich raiment, which with fast falling tears she deposited in a box at her side. In explanation the mother said, "My daughter is going away almost immediately to a distant city, to the home of her mother-in-law. It is very hard to have her go, for there she will not be kindly cared for, as she has been in her own home. I shall not know when she is in trouble; and who will comfort her?" The daughter brought her books, and took her lesson as usual, but she was very quiet. When we were leaving, she followed us a little beyond the door and said, "I do not want to go."

The lot of many of the child-wives in India is indescribably sad. In one house which we visited were two girls who had formerly been pupils in our school, one a daughter, and the other a daughter-in-law. These girls, though mere children, were considered too old to go abroad. The daughter continued her lessons at home, but the daughter-in-law was not allowed to learn, nor was she often allowed to see us. One day while giving instruction to the daughter, we saw the little child-wife at the head of a flight of stairs, looking wistfully down. "Do let her come," we pleaded. "She does not wish to come," answered the mother-in-law coldly. "Only give her permission, and she will surely come," we said. We then called to the child to come, but in vain. Then the mother-in-law called to her, and hearing her bidding her come, she came swiftly down, but with a look upon her face which it was pitiful to behold. She remained standing until the mother-in-law gave her leave to be seated. Then she dropped at our feet, and lifted up to us eyes full of fear, like those of a captured animal. A book was put into her hands that she might read. "She is too dull," said the mother-in-law, and presently she was told to go back to her duties. Then with swift steps she sped away, without casting a look behind her. Our hearts ached to see this child, so recently a happy girl in school, leading so sad a life.

Amid the wellnigh universal dread of living with a mother-in-law, it is pleasant to be able to record an incident of an opposite nature. Visiting one day a house where we had an interesting pupil, we found her sitting as usual near an older woman. When our pupil brought her books, this woman sat close beside her and followed her with her eyes as she read, looking up to us occasionally for approval. When the books were laid aside, we said something to the young woman in reference to her mother, for we took it for granted that no other relation existed between the two women than that of mother and daughter. "She is my husband's mother, but she is just the same to me as my own mother," was the young woman's response. And then she added, "That is as it should be, is it not?"

The evils of child-marriage in India are constantly witnessed. One of our pupils was particularly uninteresting, and found it difficult to make any progress in learning. No companion is this dull, ignorant woman for her keen and accomplished husband, who occupies a prominent position, and whose pursuits are entirely beyond the range of her thoughts.

There are, however, as might be expected, exceptions to the very numerous evil results which follow from child-marriage, for dull girls are not always married to bright boys, nor dull boys to bright girls.

The wife of a prominent Indian official was one of our most satisfactory pupils. She was quick at learning, and always wore a happy face. She and her husband were alike progressive. Their caste people are often shocked by the disposition they manifest to break away from the trammels of Hinduism. When remonstrated with, they are able to reply that they are both of one mind, and that irrespective of the opinions of others, they will have to do what seems to themselves to be right.

To one coming from a land, where woman is held in honor, perhaps nothing in connection with the customs of this country calls forth feelings of deeper disgust than the position accorded to her whom God made to be a helpmeet for man. The woman may be, and not unfrequently is, intellectually superior to the man to whom she is married, yet she is regarded by her husband as belonging to an inferior order of creation, and fit only to be his servant.

As far as possible, the houses in which we teach are visited during the hours when the male members of the family are absent, since the women are then more at leisure. But occasionally we encounter the master of the house.

Once on entering a house we found the husband and father sitting on the floor in native fashion, taking his morning meal. We had been allowed to enter, because a young daughter was at liberty and could go on with her lessons. The wife, standing behind her husband was waiting to serve him, while her sister, who was on a visit to the house, stood near by, ready to assist in serving, should her help be required. One or two servants were also in attendance. The master having finished his repast, water was brought, with which he cleansed first his mouth, and then his hands. When this ceremony had been performed, a compound in very general use among the natives of India, called *pán*, whose principal ingredients are the leaf of the betel-pepper and lime, was handed to him. This he took without even a glance toward the person who gave it, and stowing it away in his mouth, walked haughtily out. When the sound of his footsteps had died away, a change at once came over the scene. The wife, wearied with her work of serving, came into the court, took a seat near us, and listened to the reading, Her sister, with a sigh of relief, threw herself into a chair, and the servants went about their duties without constraint.

Not always, however, among Hindus is woman without honor. One of the houses which we visited had about it an atmosphere of home, and the wife moved about like a queen in her own domain. She was very intelligent, and a most apt pupil. She told us of the books which her husband brought to the house and read aloud to her. She rehearsed on one occasion the story of

Robinson Crusoe, which her husband had read to her, and which had fascinated her greatly.

Such a state of things is due of course to Christian example; and such cases will be multiplied as Christian influence becomes more and more felt in this land.

XIX.

EXPERIENCES WHEN ALONE IN JHANSI, AND A PILGRIMAGE TO PESHAWAR.

In September, 1888, my husband left Jhansi for Naini Tal to be present at a meeting of the Hindi New Testament Revision Committee, and was absent more than a month, while I tarried at home. A few days after his departure word was brought to me that there was sickness in the house of the native minister in the city. As soon as I could, therefore, I set out upon an errand of commiseration and relief. Taking with me medicine and such comforts as I thought might be acceptable, I stepped into the two-wheeled conveyance used by my husband, and in a case of emergency used also by me, and drove to the city. After passing through the principal gate, I went on through narrow streets and a busy bazaar until I reached the street leading to the house of the minister. At this turning, the road descended sharply, and I had but just commenced the descent when the straps holding up the shafts of my vehicle both snapped, and I was precipitated with violence to the ground. The fall rendered me insensible, and when consciousness returned I found myself supported by two Bengali gentlemen, one of whom was fanning me vigorously. Finding that my destination was the house of the native minister, they assisted me to that place, which happily was near at hand. Here my wounds were bathed in cold water, and while this was being done, the minister went in quest of a conveyance in which I could be taken home. On arriving at the bungalow, the English surgeon was sent for, and it was found that my right wrist, though not broken, was seriously injured. For a long time thereafter it was necessary to support it in a sling, and for years it remained weak. There were bruises on my head and on other parts of my body, so that for a time I suffered much, and was a forlorn-looking object. I knew that my husband's presence would not hasten my recovery, and therefore while informing him of the accident which had befallen me, I took pains not to alarm him, lest he should feel that he ought not to remain at his work. I continued to send him a few lines daily, writing with my left hand, and this new method of chirography served not only to give variety to my limited occupations, but to afford me no little amusement. In fact the experiment of writing with my left hand became so interesting and proved so successful, that I wrote to my husband that I might continue to use this hand in this service after the use of the other should be restored.

For some time before the departure of my husband for Naini Tal he had acted as chaplain to the Presbyterian soldiers, conducting a Sabbath morning service for them. Greatly to his regret it was necessary that this service should be discontinued during his absence. On the second Saturday after his departure, as I was reclining in a long invalid chair, word was brought to me that two soldiers belonging to the Scotch Battery had come, and desired an interview with me. Under the circumstances I was decidedly adverse to receiving them, and asked that they would kindly excuse me. When this message was conveyed to the men, they returned answer that they had come on important business, and *must* see me. They were therefore admitted.

I saw at once that they were laboring under excitement. After expressing regret at my condition, and apologising for the intrusion, one of the men said, "We *had* to come; for we are in great trouble, and we felt sure that you could help us." With some embarrassment the man deputed to present the case thus began: "As you know, Ma'am, we are law-abiding. We do not drink, we are never in the guard-house, at least have never been there until now, and in all things we try to conduct ourselves as soldiers of the Queen should. We are in church regularly, as you can testify, Ma'am. Well, the first Saturday after Mr. Holcomb went away, we were notified that during the absence of the Presbyterian chaplain the Presbyterian soldiers would be required to attend the parade service of the Church of England. We protested respectfully, saying that they had no right to compel us to attend an Episcopal service, as we were Presbyterians. Our Captain replied that there were but two *religions*, the Church of England and the Roman Catholic." Then in a tone of great vehemence the soldier continued, "But he had no right to say that. Our fathers in the old country and in the olden time suffered for their faith, and we will show them that we too are ready to suffer. Well, when Sunday came we were marched to the Church of England, but we refused to enter, and marched back to our barracks. For this act of insubordination, we were put into the guard-house, a new experience for us, Ma'am. But we had acted conscientiously, so we did not regret what we had done. We wondered during the week what would be done the next Sunday. Well, this morning we were again notified that during the absence of the Presbyterian chaplain the Presbyterian soldiers would be required to attend the services of the Church of England. We are determined to resist, because we feel that we are in the right. We will suffer rather than yield to injustice. We have come to you, Ma'am, feeling that in some way you will surely be able to help us."

'In what way do you think I can aid you?' I asked. "We do not know, Ma'am; but there is no one else to whom we can go for advice." Then after a moment of hesitation, he said, "Could you not write to the English chaplain and ask him to excuse us?"

'I am afraid that would hardly do,' I answered. 'Would it not be better for you, during the absence of Mr. Holcomb to attend the services of the Church of England, as you are requested to do?'

"We cannot do that, Ma'am. It is a matter of principle. They have no right to compel us to do that, and we are determined to resist."

His face was flushed, and there was a look of such fierce determination on that rugged Scotch countenance that I knew it would be useless further to counsel submission. I therefore said, 'I cannot now see any way out of the difficulty. I will take time for reflection, and if I can do anything for you, rest assured that it will be done.' My soldier friends then left me.

After much thought and prayer I resolved to send a letter to the officer in command of the garrison, putting the whole case before him. I knew that he might regard such an act as quite outside my province, as indeed it was, but it seemed the only course to pursue. So with my left hand, as yet unskilled in use of the pen, I sent to this officer a note telling him what had transpired. I reminded him that these men now apparently so mutinous, had hitherto borne a good character; that in the present case their resistance arose from a feeling that unlawful authority was being exercised; that it was painful to them to take such a stand as they had done, but it was with them a matter of principle. They had waited until the end of the week before reporting the matter, to see if the order of the preceding week would be repeated; then in their extremity they had come to me for advice. I told him that although during the absence of my husband the Sabbath morning service would be discontinued, an evening service conducted by a layman would be maintained, and the Presbyterian soldiers would not therefore be left entirely without the means of grace.

I sent away this letter with many misgivings. Two or three hours after the despatch of the note, a tall orderly in livery appeared, and making a profound salaam, handed in the reply upon which so much depended. With eager haste I opened the note. The commandant after thanking me for writing so fully and so frankly, said, "I have given orders that during the absence from the station of the acting Presbyterian chaplain, the Presbyterian soldiers are not to be compelled to attend the services of the Church of England."

As speedily as possible the purport of this communication was made known to the anxious soldiers, who rejoiced, as did I, over so happy a termination of what had threatened to be serious in its consequences.

Had the officer in command not been a true gentleman, he might have resented my interference, and felt that the men richly merited punishment. They were quite right in thinking that it was unlawful to compel them to attend the services of the Church of England. They had acted wrongly in marching back to their barracks without permission. They should have waited outside the church until the close of the service, and then marched back with the other soldiers of the garrison.

Those Scotch soldiers were fine manly fellows, knowing the Bible well, and it was a pleasure to minister to them in spiritual things.

On my husband's return from Naini Tal soon after the middle of October, I was able to be about as usual. I had, however, been much shaken by the accident and consequent suffering, and when in November my husband was obliged to leave home again to attend the meeting of the Synod of India, to be held in Ambala, he was unwilling to leave me alone at home, and I accordingly accompanied him.

After spending two or three days at the Synod, I resolved for the sake of further change, to visit some of the mission stations of the north. I first paid a short visit to Ludhiana, a place full of interest because of the various kinds of mission work in progress there, both in connection with our own Board, and the "Society for Promoting Female Education in the East." The ladies of this society work in co-operation with our mission, and consequently the missionary work in Ludhiana is *one* in the most real sense. Six months of the first year of our life in India had been spent in Ludhiana, and it was most encouraging to note the progress which had been made since 1870 in all departments of work.

Proceeding northward I passed by Lahore, as our missionaries of that station were in attendance on the meetings of the Synod and the mission in Ambala. Two or three delightful days were spent in Rawal Pindi, then the frontier station of the Ludhiana Mission. Subsequently this station was transferred to the American United Presbyterian Mission.

I had long desired to see Peshawar, not only because it is in itself a very interesting city and well worthy of a visit, but because it had at one time been a station of our mission, and work had been begun there under circumstances of peculiar interest. It was hoped that missionaries might from this point penetrate into Afghanistan, then closed, and still closed to the Gospel messenger. For beginning a work among the Afghans under the auspices of our Board, Major Conran gave fifteen thousand rupees, and the Rev. Isidor Loewenthal was the missionary selected for this post. While preaching to the people of the city of Peshawar and its vicinity in the Urdu and Persian languages, he was also busily employed in the study of Pushtu, the language of the Afghans, in order that he might begin as soon as possible to translate the Word of God into this language. He had completed the translation of the New Testament into Pushtu when he met his tragic death.

It is an easy journey by rail from Rawal Pindi to Peshawar, and arrangements having been made for my entertainment at the latter place, in case I should be able to go there, I felt that this was an opportunity for the realisation of a long cherished desire. On my arrival at the railway station in Peshawar, I was met by one of the ladies of the Church of England Zenana Mission, and driven to the home of these ladies in the heart of the native city. Their unique dwelling had formerly been a caravanserai. The large rambling house was situated on a rise of ground, and not only afforded a good view of the city, but commanded an extensive prospect. The green valley of Peshawar with its encircling hills was very beautiful.

All the foreign residences, and the British garrison, are situated at some distance from the native city.

The Rev. Robert Clark of the Church Missionary Society, who was the pioneer missionary in Peshawar, had purchased the caravanserai in the city, and had suggested that it might be utilised as a missionary residence, since the Afghans, though wild and turbulent, are yet a sociable people, and would be likely to avail themselves of opportunities for intercourse with missionaries residing in the city, especially if they were familiar with Pushtu. Peshawar is a walled city, and within these walls shutting out all western civilisation, and shutting in a fanatical Asiatic population, few Europeans cared to trust themselves after nightfall. It was not strange therefore that none of the early missionaries wished to reside in the city. Even the native minister was averse to living there. He, however, gave as a reason for his objection, that the place was insanitary! But after the zenana mission had begun work in Peshawar, the ladies of this society felt the inconvenience of living outside the city, and proposed to take up their residence inside the walls. This proposition did not commend itself to the other missionaries, but as the ladies were urgent in the matter, a trial was permitted.

At the time of my visit these ladies of the zenana mission had been a long time domiciled in the old caravanserai. Hanging on the wall of one of the rooms, neatly framed, was this text from *The Lamentations of Jeremiah*, the fourth chapter, twentieth verse.—

"*Under his shadow we shall live among the heathen.*"

One of the members of this zenana mission was a medical lady, and she found it convenient to be within easy call of those to whose needs she desired to minister. The zenana teachers and their assistants found it equally convenient to be near their pupils and the schools which they superintended. The people, they all said, seemed gratified that they were willing to trust themselves to live in their midst.

The peoples inhabiting the borderland of North India are thus described by one who knew them well :—" These tribes are savages—noble savages perhaps—and not without some tincture of virtue and generosity, but still absolutely barbarians. They have nothing approaching to government or civil institutions. In their eyes the one great commandment is blood for blood, and fire and sword for all people not Mahomedans. They are thievish and predatory to the last degree. For gold they will do almost everything except betray a guest." May it not be that these wild people of Peshawar consider these defenceless women, who are living in their midst only to do them good, as in some sense their guests, and therefore refrain from doing them harm? At all events these missionary ladies, "abiding under the shadow of the Almighty," have these many years lived in the city of Peshawar in perfect safety. While this is a fact worthy of very special notice, it is also true that about the time when plans were being made for beginning missionary work in Peshawar, the highest British official, connected with the civil station there, was assassinated by one of these blood-thirsty hillmen. Though, as I have said, the murder of this officer occurred near the time when plans for missionary work in Peshawar were being formed, yet there was no connection whatever between the two events.

One morning while in Peshawar I visited the beautiful cemetery in the civil station, and stood beside the grave of that servant of the Lord, who had been cut off in his prime and when to human ken his life-work seemed to be but just begun. The monument above his grave bore this inscription :—

To the memory of Rev. Isidor Loewenthal, of the American Presbyterian Mission, who translated the New Testament into Pushtu. He was shot by his chaukidar, April 27th, 1864.

"I am not ashamed of the Gospel of Christ, for it is the power of God unto salvation to every one that believeth."—Romans i. 16.

In a beautiful Christian sanctuary, which was erected in Peshawar some years after the death of Mr. Loewenthal, I found a tablet to his memory. These marble memorials may disappear, but the Word of God which he translated into the vernacular of the Afghan people will be an enduring memorial.

I left Peshawar in time to meet my husband in Ambala at the close of the Synod and the Mission meetings, and together we returned to Jhansi.

XX.

A SITE SECURED FOR A CHURCH IN THE CITY.

Being anxious to secure as soon as possible a site for a church in the city we had for some time been on the lookout for an eligible situation. The right location of a mission church is a matter of no small importance, and we desired that no mistake should be made in taking this step. At length we found a small plot of vacant ground which we thought would answer our purpose, and the owner seemed willing to sell it, but finally refused to part with it, and we were much disappointed. A better position was, however, afterwards secured.

One day while passing along the main thoroughfare leading to the heart of the city, my husband's attention was attracted to a small plot of ground, triangular in shape, close to the Rani's palace. Covered with debris, and overgrown with thistles and other noxious weeds, the ground did not present an attractive appearance, but the position seemed an admirable one for a church. The street on which it fronted was not a babel, as were the bazars of the city, though it was a much-frequented highway. The more we looked at this site, the more we liked it. It seemed most desirable in every respect. On making inquiry in regard to it, we found that it belonged to the government. Formerly, houses for the priests connected with the palace had stood upon it. Those houses had been destroyed after the mutiny, as the property had been confiscated. My husband made known to the magistrate his desire to purchase this site, if possible, and this official, who was our neighbor and friend, said he would see what could be done; but a considerable time elapsed before any thing further was heard about it. The magistrate had not, however, forgotten the matter. One day he accosted my husband, while passing him in the city, and said to him, "I think we can let you have that piece of land, if you still want it." "I do want it," replied my husband; whereupon the magistrate asked, "In what way would you like to acquire it." "In any way and on any terms," said my husband. "Would it suit you to take it on a lease of ninety-nine years?" was then asked. To this question an affirmative answer was given, whereupon the magistrate said he would recommend that such a lease be given.

It was necessary, that he should refer the matter to his superior, the commissioner, and in case he approved of the proposal, it would go to the Lieutenant-Governor of these provinces for his sanction. When the proposal reached the commissioner, instead of approving of it, he suggested that a more satisfactory way in which to dispose of the land would be to sell it at auction to the highest bidder. The government could not then be charged with favoring the Christians, as Hindus and Mahomedans would have the same opportunity to purchase it as the Christian missionary.

When informed that in accordance with the commissioner's recommendation the land would be sold at auction, we were disappointed, for we feared that in order to secure it we might be obliged to pay a large price for it, and, besides, there was the possibility that we might fail to obtain it on any terms. We had no reason to think that either Hindus or Mahomedans would buy it merely to prevent it from falling into our hands, nevertheless we felt no little anxiety concerning the result of the auction sale.

It was advertised that the sale would take place at the magistrate's court on a certain date, and my husband thought it would be advisable to be present himself at the auction, rather than to depute another to act for him. Accordingly he went to the court at the appointed time, and found the magistrate ready to proceed with the sale. A few persons from the city were present to make bids, and when the auction began. these were left for a time to bid against each other, my husband in the meantime remaining silent. An amazingly small bid was at first made, and the subsequent increments were of the same character. This was entirely in accordance with native custom, for their bargaining of any sort always proceeds with the utmost caution and deliberation. To the average oriental, time is of little consequence. In buying or selling he carefully avoids any manifestation of undue interest in the transaction.

After a time my husband interposed a bid, and by his offer enhanced somewhat the rate of increase in the bidding. His offer was exceeded by the bid of another, but he promptly made another considerable advance. This seemed to convince the others that he was determined to have the land, and there was a pause in the bidding, upon which the magistrate closed the sale by declaring that the land belonged to Mr. Holcomb, the price to be paid being one hundred and ninety rupees, or about sixty-five dollars! This purchase gave us a freehold possession of the ground, exempt from taxation of any kind. The result of the auction sale was favorable beyond our most sanguine expectation. The interference of the commissioner on behalf of the general public had very materially aided our cause. It was not until after the sale was concluded, that those who had taken any interest in it awaked to the realisation of a lost opportunity. They would then gladly have purchased the property at a greatly enhanced price, but to their chagrin their advances were unavailing, as the land was no longer in the market. The site proved to be the very best position in the city for our church.

XXI.

SECULAR AFFAIRS.

To no small extent missionaries in the foreign field are necessarily occupied with what may be designated secular affairs, for how much soever they may desire to be absorbed with interests which are wholly spiritual, they find that in practical missionary work material concerns play a very important part. In beginning work in a new mission field, where land must be obtained, buildings erected, and plans formed for the prosecution of various kinds of work, it is absolutely unavoidable that unremitting attention should be given to what we call in Hindustani "bandobast," or arrangements in general. Of his engagements in 1889 my husband wrote near the end of that year, "There was hardly a day when my mind was free from cares concerning some negotiation pending, or some work of building or planning which was in progress." Confined as he was to the station by such occupations, he was unable to do any work in the district during the cold season. We were therefore especially thankful that at the beginning of this year our small staff of workers was increased by the transfer from Fatehpur of catechist Dharm Singh and his wife. Dharm Singh had been in the mission from his boyhood, having been received as an orphan. He had been well proved as a worker, and possessed such qualities as peculiarly fitted him for service in a new field, prominent among which was the faculty of making friends among the people. Both he and his wife were ever ready to welcome to their house all sorts of visitors, and to extend hospitality to any Christian wayfarer. The coming of this catechist made it possible for a fair amount of work to be done in the district during the cold season of this year. The two brethren, the minister and the catechist, made two tours together, being absent from the station forty-six days. They went as far as Lalitpur, fifty-five miles to the south of Jhansi, and as far as Mau-Ranipur, forty miles to the east, preaching to attentive audiences, and leaving behind them Christian tracts and portions of Scripture in the towns and villages visited.

A matter which caused my husband no little trouble at the beginning of this year was the settlement of the boundary lines of the mission compound. A tract of land comprising twenty-one acres belonged to the house which had been purchased. In former days land was little worth in Jhansi, and consequently the settlement of boundary lines and the fencing of compounds in the civil station had not by some of the property holders been considered essential. Now that land was becoming more valuable, the most careful attention was being paid by land-owners to the securing of their rights. Moreover the municipal authorities had made it obligatory upon all owners of property in the civil station to enclose their compounds with stone walls or wire fencing within a specified time. As far as we were concerned, this order instead of being regarded as an unnecessary imposition, was welcomed as affording us most opportune assistance, for in order to get rid of various annoyances, some of which were becoming intolerable, it was absolutely essential that precisely that should be done which we were now required to do. Our compound, quadrangular in shape, had a stone wall on the side facing the road leading to the city, and was open to the public on the other three sides. The boundaries of the compound were not so clearly marked that any one could be called to account for trespassing, and so horsemen galloped over the ground, vehicles of all sorts traversed the premises, and cattle grazed upon the land, at will.

One road through our grounds which was much used by the public was that which led from the railway station directly to the city; and from this thoroughfare other roads led into adjoining compounds. Our neighbors especially would be inconvenienced, and the general public might feel aggrieved by our closing these short-cuts through our premises. By its stringent order, therefore, the municipality had come to our aid, and we were thankful that while doing that which would so greatly benefit ourselves, we should be able to say to any one who might think that his privileges were being curtailed, that in doing what we had a perfect right to do, we also acted under the compulsion of the government. As we proceeded to carry out the order of the authorities, happily circumstances greatly favored us. The thoroughfare just spoken of, ran not only through our compound, but also through ground occupied by the government police, and the police officer was as anxious as we were to have that thoroughfare closed. Just at the right time all difficulty as regarded the inconveniencing of our other neighbors by the closing of this road was avoided by their removal to another part of the station.

The next obstacle which confronted us was not

removed without tedious and vexatious negotiations, and the expenditure of a considerable amount of money. A number of huts belonging to a Mahomedan stood partly on ground belonging to the compound which we now owned. This had come about by encroachment, and mere lapse of time had sufficed to establish a proprietary right to the ground. Not only had our undesirable neighbor encroached in the past by building on ground which was not his, but he now asserted that a considerable portion of our compound also belonged to him by reason of the fact that the doors of his huts opened towards it, and that it had for a long time been used by him. This claim could not, however, be substantiated, but it illustrates the character of the unprincipled Asiatic. To have such a neighbor, or rather neighbors (for the huts swarmed with suchlike Moslem occupants), was not to be endured, if they could be dispossessed, and they were finally bought out for about $ 333. Our compound wall on this side was then so built as to include the huts, which when repaired and renovated were utilised as teachers' quarters.

Yet another difficulty arose as the work of enclosing the compound was approaching completion. The negligence of the former owners of the property in not looking after their boundary, had caused a serious mistake to be made in marking the limit of the compound on the municipal map, and this mistake, had it not been discovered, would have resulted in depriving us of several acres of ground. The true boundary having been shown to my husband, further inquiry on his part had elicited the information that an old map existed which would show the correct delimitation of the land. Obtaining this map he found that the boundary line as shown upon it agreed entirely with the somewhat obscure earthen embankment which had been pointed out to him as the real limit of the compound. Having ascertained where the true boundary was, we were planning to change the position of a gateway, when an attempt was made by a native official to prevent us from carrying out our design, and our work was arrested until the matter could come before the British magistrate for settlement. At the time appointed for the adjustment of the matter, the municipal map was exhibited as proving conclusively that our entrance, if placed where we wished to place it, would extend beyond the boundary of the compound. But unknown to our antagonist my husband had in his possession the older map already mentioned. It bore, moreover, the government stamp, and its reliability could not therefore be impugned. This was shown to the magistrate, and a brief examination served to convince him that it indicated the limit of our land correctly, and consequently there could be no objection to our having our entrance as we had planned to have it. To the confusion of the official who had sought to thwart our purpose, he then and there authorised my husband to proceed with the work which on the preceding day had been arrested. In this incident oriental duplicity is exemplified, for our antagonist was no other than the very man who had previously shown us the true boundary of our land.

To see our broad domain entirely enclosed was an immense satisfaction, and during the years which have elapsed since this work was completed, the wall has been an unspeakable boon. For a mission compound in India roominess is desirable, but not always obtainable. Our "Rehoboth" was within our reach at the time it was purchased, because then property in Jhansi was inexpensive. In fact the land cost us practically nothing, as the buildings were worth the price of the whole property, which was somewhat less than $3,000. It will be more and more valuable to us as the years go by and our work extends.

XXII.

PLANS FOR A CHURCH AND READING-ROOM.

How a choice site for our church and reading-room in the city was secured has been already told. As soon as possible after this ground had been purchased we began to make plans for the erection of our building. As no funds for this purpose were in hand, it seemed to us that it would be the part of wisdom to plan for present necessities only. Our scheme therefore was a very modest one. All that we at first thought of building was a comparatively small and plain structure which would answer for church purposes, and could also be used as a public reading-room during the week, and which would cost about $ 2,000. As there were two high schools for boys in Jhansi, there seemed to be no demand for a third one, and even had we wished to establish such a school, there was no money for the purpose. But we desired by some means to reach the educated young men of the place, who could be counted not merely by scores, but by hundreds. We therefore determined to provide a reading-room for their benefit, having on a visit to some of the mission stations in South India seen how useful such an institution can be made as a missionary agency. For our combined church and reading-room we planned to have a building not more than forty or fifty feet in length, and twenty or twenty-five feet in width, with a veranda along the entire front, taking for our model one of the plainest and least expensive houses which the railway company was building for its employees. The plan for such a structure was drawn at our request by an architect in Allahabad, who had on other occasions been employed by the mission; and his sketch, with a rough estimate of the cost of the building, was, according to custom, circulated among the members of the mission for their approval or disapproval. While some expressed their approval of the plan proposed, others objected to it, saying that the building looked like a barrack rather than a church edifice, and that as it was designed for a church, it ought to have an ecclesiastical appearance.

It was an auspicious circumstance that very soon after the circular had gone its round of the different stations, a special business meeting of the mission was held in Allahabad. An opportunity was thus afforded of coming to some definite conclusion concerning the Jhansi church scheme. Before they separated, the members of the mission were entirely at one in reference to this matter, and their agreement came about in this way. While they were engaged in discussing the plan which had been proposed in the circular, the architect who had drawn up this plan called at the house where they were assembled, to have an interview with one of their number concerning another matter of business. Having been told how opportunely he had appeared in their midst, the architect was then informed that the plan of the building which had been submitted to the mission had not met the entire approval of all the members, and he was asked to draw while there a rough sketch of a church with a reading-room attached, the whole to be adapted to the plot of ground on which it was to stand, and which he himself had seen. In a very short time the sketch was ready, and all after seeing it said, "This is what we want." By general consent the dimensions of the building were considerably increased, as it was thought wise to provide not merely for present but for prospective needs. The building was so planned that the two rooms could, whenever desired, be used as one audience room. The architect thought that such a building as was contemplated might be erected at a cost of about $3,000, and the expenditure of such a sum seemed to the mission entirely justifiable.

XXIII.

FIRST ANNUAL MEETING OF THE MISSION IN JHANSI, AND THE LAYING OF THE CORNER-STONE OF THE CHURCH.

When we began in May 1889 to clear the ground in preparation for building our church, a remarkable interest in our proceeding was manifested by some of the people in the city. Rumors were rife that the excavations about to be made would reveal buried treasure, but so far were such expectations unfulfilled that not even a single copper coin was unearthed. Two rusty gun-barrels and a sword-blade were, however, turned up. It is possible that in the terrible conflict of the troops of General Sir Hugh Rose with the rebel sepoys on the 3rd of April, 1858, these weapons may have been used against the British.

To the casual observer the work on the church foundations may have appeared to advance very slowly, but to any one who cared to inspect it, the progress made from time to time could not but have seemed very substantial, for the labor and expense connected with this initial portion of the building proved to be vastly greater than had been anticipated, on account of the depth of excavation which was found to be necessary in order to reach solid ground. We hoped to be able at the annual meeting of the mission, which was to be held in Jhansi in November, to lay the corner-stone of this edifice with appropriate ceremonies, and consequently bent our energies to the accomplishment of this end.

It was a great pleasure to us to welcome the members of the mission to this station, many of whom saw it for the first time on this occasion. The main line of the Indian Midland Railway System had been completed, linking the Great Indian Peninsula Railway in the south-west with the railways in the north and north-east *via* Jhansi, so that our friends coming to us from Allahabad, or by the way of Cawnpore or Agra could enjoy quick transit by rail, instead of enduring, as we had often done, an uncomfortable and tedious journey by the old-time *dák gárí*.

The degree of personl interest felt by us in the completion of the main line of the Indian Midland Railway may be understood by my mentioning that when the first passenger train was to leave Jhansi for Bombay, we drove down to the station, a distance of two miles, at midnight to see it "pull out." After it had vanished in the darkness we returned to our bungalow with a feeling of elation because that we in the heart of India were now linked by rail with the great seaport through which our weekly news from the home land reached us.

All our missionaries who could come were present at this annual meeting, which was in some respects a memorable one. At this time was inaugurated the devotional hour, preceding breakfast and the usual prayer with which the work of each day began. Those early morning meetings proved so profitable spiritually that they have ever since been continued at our annual gatherings.

JHANSI RAILWAY STATION.

The business sessions which occupied the greater part of each day were held in my husband's study, an unusually large room. The central room of the bungalow which was our sitting-room, was the social rallying place. In two rooms adjoining the sitting-room, and having each a veranda, was spread our common table. In two remaining rooms some of our guests were accommodated at night, but the majority were quartered in tents pitched in the compound. According to custom our evenings were occupied with the reading and hearing of reports from the various stations.

Our annual mission meetings generally continue about the same length of time as the sittings of our General Assembly at home. No greater mistake could be made than to suppose that missionaries in foreign lands are essentially different from Christian workers in the home department of the great harvest field. It need not therefore excite wonder that, following the example of those who seek to provide in some way restful recreation for the members of our General Assemblies, we had planned that at some time during the meeting at Jhansi our friends should enjoy with us an excursion to the Barwa Sagar castle and lake. That something of this sort is not more commonly done by us here in India is doubtless largely due to the fact that there is very little which is worth seeing in the immediate vicinity of most of our stations. Jhansi, however, being unique in respect of its having near at hand a variety of places worthy of a visit, we resolved to improve the opportunity which our situation at this new station afforded, of taking what would be for us all an entirely new departure.

The excursion to Barwa Sagar could be made either by rail or the macadamised road. The latter was chosen, as it would afford us more freedom and more enjoyment.

On the day appointed for the outing we started early in the morning in a variety of conveyances, the most comfortable of which were reserved for the ladies, and a drive of eight miles brought us to the river Betwa. Here ferry-boats of the most primitive style, propelled by diminutive paddles, conveyed our vehicles and ourselves across a broad expanse of water artificially created. At the distance of seventeen miles from the point where we crossed the river a strong stone embankment, stopping the flow of a comparatively small river, forms the lake which is used as a feeder to a great irrigation system.

Although we were more than half an hour in crossing by the ferry, the time was none too long for the enjoyment of the quiet movement of the boats, and the rare beauty of the scene on either bank, and up and down the river as far as the eye could see. On disembarking we again took our places in our vehicles and were driven a distance of three miles by a beautifully shaded road to the castle by the lake-side. On one side, the fields irrigated by the water from the lake were beautifully green, while great tamarind and mango trees and lofty palms adorned the landscape. In the morning sun the placid lake shone like a mirror, its rocky island appeared like a gem on its surface, and charming were the views of its wooded shore, the fantastic piles of rock beyond, and the distant hills. The old castle, and the wonderful stone embankment of the lake, furnished completeness to the scene, which in the opinion of all who enjoyed it that day, surpassed anything they had ever beheld on the plains of India.

When for the time being our friends were satisfied with seeing, all were called to breakfast, which was served in one of the upper rooms of the castle. Following breakfast we assembled for "family prayers," and

FERRY BOAT ON THE BETWA.

probably never before within those walls had so large a company united their voices in praising God. In a pavilion, built on a terrace overlooking the lake, the gentlemen met for a business session, and thus on this memorable day work and pleasure were combined. After luncheon a part of the company spent an hour or more in strolling about the beautiful park-like expanse, while others found enjoyment in boating on the lake. Returning we reached Jhansi just as the darkness came on, and when in the mission bungalow we gathered around the table for the evening meal, tired though some of the number were, there was not one who did not feel that the day had been well spent.

The crowning event of this first mission meeting in Jhansi was the laying of the corner-stone of the church in the city. This ceremony took place on the afternoon of the 21st of November. On the level space within the foundation walls, which were then a little above the ground, cotton carpets had been spread, upon which the members of the mission, and a few friends who were interested in our work, took their seats in chairs which had been provided for them. On the higher ground opposite the church-site great numbers of people from the city hearing that something unusual was to be done had assembled. Soon the road was entirely blocked by the crowd, but no inconvenience seemed to arise from this, as all passers-by were ready to join the multitude of spectators who were eager to witness the ceremony about to take place. The exercises consisted of prayers, the reading of passages of Scripture, the singing of a hymn prepared for the occasion, and brief addresses, all being in Hindustani, except the hymn which was in English.

The on-lookers were told that on the foundation which

had been laid was to be erected a temple to the living God, a sanctuary for God's worship, to which all would be welcomed. It was to be built in their midst, because it was intended for the use of the people of the city of Jhansi. The corner-stone was then swung into its place and "duly laid," the doxology was sung, and the majority of the missionary party returned to the mission house, while a few remained some time longer to preach to the large audience which the novel circumstances had brought together.

The laying of the corner-stone of God's house within the walls of this heathen city was an event full of interest to all who had participated in the exercises connected with it, and to us who had toiled in preparation for it, it was a time full of promise for the future. The inscription on the corner-stone is this,

"*Other foundation can no man lay*
than that which is laid, which is
JESUS CHRIST."

An incident belonging to this occasion, which touched us deeply, must here be recorded. Before leaving us to return to their homes our friends unsolicited presented us with a generous sum of money, their gift to us to aid in the erection of this "house of prayer."

XXIV.

PROGRESS IN VARIOUS DIRECTIONS.

On the 5th of March, 1890, in accordance with the direction of the Presbytery of Allahabad a Church was organised in Jhansi, and catechist Dharm Singh was chosen ruling elder. Such was the outward beginning of the spiritual House of God—the Church of the living God—intended to be the pillar and ground of the truth in the midst of this heathen city.

As to the material structure in which God's people were to assemble for his worship, and in which his truth was to be proclaimed and his ordinances dispensed, with the exception of a few months when the work was suspended for lack of bricks, its growth went on apace. During its construction there was hardly a day when it was not necessary for my husband to watch the work, lest it should not be properly done, and lest bad materials should be used. This entailed a very heavy and constant burden of care, in the bearing of which he enjoyed the satisfaction of knowing that the work throughout was well done, which in itself was no slight reward. The main part of the work was carried out by contract, and while the European contractors who resided in Allahabad were honorable men and desired that the work should be well done, the sub-contractors who did the work, and the persons employed to look after it, were not so much concerned to advance our interests as their own. Consequently on several occasions it was necessary to suspend operations, because the work was not being satisfactorily done, and to await directions from the contractors in Allahabad, after representations had been sent to them both by my husband and those who were doing the work; and to the credit of the European firm it is a pleasure to be able to say that they invariably accepted my husband's statements implicitly, and gave orders that his wishes should be complied with; and this was done notwithstanding that their principal agent in Jhansi was of the same nationality as themselves. My husband received valuable assistance from time to time from a number of English engineers residing in Jhansi. During an entire month when he was absent from home while the foundations were being laid, a royal engineer frequently inspected the work. This assistance was all the more prized because it was gratuitously given.

"We must sometime have a tower for our church," we had said; and the architect's plan of the building included a tower with a spire; but when we began to build we did not see our way to carry out the entire plan. In the hope, however, that the tower might sometime be built we had been advised to lay the foundation for it. But not until the walls of the church began to rise did we decide to do this. The place for the tower was at the angle where the church and the veranda of the reading-room joined, and here we sank deep down in the earth a solid mass of concrete sufficient to sustain any weight which might be put upon it. It was well that we decided to do so, for contributions came to us in such generous measure that at length we were able to authorise the contractors to complete the building according to the original scheme. Our spire made our church, after the old fortress, the most conspicuous landmark in the city. "It is impossible to get out of sight of that spire," the Hindustani people say. It can be seen from afar by people approaching the city. When strangers coming to Jhansi see our church tower with its graceful spire pointing heavenward, and ask what it is, they are told that this is the place where the Christians meet to worship God, and so our tower stands in the midst of pinnacled heathen temples and minaretted mosques, a constant witness to the true and living God.

When the contract for building the church was given, it was expressly stipulated that no work should be done on the Lord's day. On the opposite side of the road from our church, hospital buildings were being erected by the government at the same time that our church was being built, and work on these buildings went on without cessation during the seven days of the week, while the work on our church was regularly suspended from Saturday night until Monday morning. Our regard for the Christian Sabbath was thus very markedly shown, and that God's blessing was with us was very manifest, for although women and children were employed in carrying bricks and mortar for the work on the walls and the tower, and were constantly ascending and descending on ladders which, as they were made of bamboo sticks and strings, had frequently to be repaired, yet during the progress of the entire work no one was in any way injured.

The plot of land on which our church was built was large enough to afford room for the walls of our structure, but neither on the front side, nor in the rear, was more space left than was needed for a narrow footpath, and at first there seemed to be no prospect for the enlargement of the ground in any direction. Contrary to our expectation, however, we were in due time able to secure all the additions which either our cramped position seemed to require, or which for our greater comfort were much to be desired. These additions were obtained not all at one time, nor through a single official, but at different times, and through various officials, as circumstances opened the way. The first addition obtained was a strip of ground twelve feet in width at the rear of the building. This acquisition was of the greatest importance, as it secured the removal of huts and a cattle-pound whose close proximity to us was most objectionable. This addition was soon extended at one end to the width of fifteen feet, and at the other end to a much greater width. Then toward the road our boundary was finally fixed at the distance of eleven feet from one corner, and about forty feet from the other. This was a very special favor, as the result of this enlargement was the narrowing of the public road. Lastly, we were able to secure on a fifty years' lease the entire plot of land at the rear of the church, averaging about one hundred and twenty feet in width, and extending to the public road, a distance of two hundred feet. This clear space, affording us a sufficient compound, was made over to us by the government on condition of our paying for the use of it the sum of four dollars per annum!

The crowning event of the year 1890 was the addition to our staff of a missionary and his wife—the Rev. H. D. and Mrs. Griswold—a greatly desiderated and much needed reinforcement. Mr. and Mrs. Griswold reached India in time to be present at the annual meeting of the mission which was held in Etawah in November, and at our urgent request, and to our great joy, were appointed to Jhansi. They accompanied us when we returned to our station, and lived with us for three months, after which time they took up their abode in their own hired house.

Mr. and Mrs. Griswold within a year after their arrival in India were able to engage in evangelistic work in the villages of the district, and they found this work most interesting and encouraging. They were accompanied by catechist Dharm Singh, who has always shown great zeal in this work.

The work in the district ought to be carried on uninterruptedly during five or six months of each year by a missionary specially set apart for it, and aided by native preachers; and during the remainder of the year, when it might not be possible on account of the great heat to prosecute this work continuously as in the cooler weather, frequent visits could be made to those villages where any special interest in the Gospel message had been manifested. It stands to reason that the work in the station and in the district can never be effectively prosecuted by a single-handed missionary. Were the one missionary able to divide himself into two, then it might be possible to multiply his efforts, but as he cannot be in two places at the same time, one work must necessarily suffer while he is engaged elsewhere in another. It is in vain therefore to exhort him to make up, by increased effort, for the paucity of help as yet furnished by the Church at home, when he is already accomplishing in one sphere all that he is able to do. For each of our central stations with its surrounding district at least two missionaries should be provided. It is therefore the earnest hope of the mission that we may be speedily reinforced all along the line, that the battle with heathenism may be fought more successfully, and that the victory for Christ on the fields we have chosen may be the sooner achieved.

During the cold season of 1890-91 we were favored with a visit from Mr. W. H. Grant of New York. It is always a pleasure to us to receive visits from pilgrims from the home land, if they are in sympathy with us and our work. Mr. Grant was such a visitor. On one of the days when he was with us we went to the city to see the sculptured stone, weighing several hundred pounds, intended for the pinnacle of the church spire, lifted to its place. The hero of this by no means insignificant achievement was a Swede, who had been employed by us as a day-laborer for some time. After the stone had been successfully placed in the position for which it was designed, and all who had been engaged in the operation of elevating and adjusting this top-stone of our spire had safely descended to the ground, the missionaries of the station, together with Mr. Grant and the Rev. Nabibakhsh, gathered under a tree near by and sang the long metre doxology. Mr. Grant then photographed the unfinished church, and the picture which he took as a memento of this interesting occasion is reproduced in this book.

CHURCH IN COURSE OF ERECTION.

XXV.

AN ENGLISH LIBRARY OBTAINED FOR OUR READING-ROOM.

We had resolved to make the reading-room as inviting as possible, and we therefore regarded a good English library as an indispensable requisite. Of infidel and impure literature which is accessible to English readers in India, much of which is even thrust in the way of young men, there is no lack. To place wholesome and instructive reading within reach of the educated and English-speaking young men of Jhansi seemed therefore very desirable. Many young Indians who have but an imperfect knowledge of English are fond of pondering over English books, and of those who have pursued English studies in the schools, not to say the colleges, there are not a few who are able to appreciate almost any English book which may be placed in their hands.

As we had no money with which to purchase such books as we desired to obtain, our only resource was to seek to interest in our enterprise those who could aid us with their contributions. Letters giving full information in regard to our mission station, and the agencies we were employing and desired to employ for promoting the well-being of different classes of the people were accordingly addressed to a number of individuals and Churches in different parts of the world, to whom we were known, and also to a number of religious societies and publishing houses in the United States and Great Britain; and beyond our most sanguine expectations, sympathetic and generous responses were promptly received. I cannot now recall a single refusal to comply with my request for aid. The officers of one or two Societies did indeed at first write that while they were deeply interested in our project, they greatly regretted that the rules of their Societies would not permit them to make us free grants of books; but in each of these cases a second letter followed the first, saying that the circumstances were so exceptional that they had decided that their rules might be relaxed in our favor.

One or two thoughtful friends not only made liberal gifts themselves, but in their replies to my communications mentioned other persons to whom application might be made with good hope of success.

An English lady, the widow of a military officer who had spent a number of years in India when her husband was connected with the Indian army, whose acquaintance we had made in the Waldensian Valleys while taking our first furlough, when informed of what we were attempting in the way of obtaining a library of English books for our reading-room, expressed great interest in our undertaking, and secured for us a fine collection of choice fresh volumes.

The people of the Cairns Memorial Presbyterian Church of Melbourne, to whom we were in other ways deeply indebted for help in carrying on our work, sent us a box of books.

All the contributors cannot here be mentioned. It may suffice to say that before the end of the year we had obtained a library of more than one thousand volumes of valuable books, and that to all the contributors, whether individuals, or Societies, or Churches, or publishing houses letters conveying our grateful thanks were sent.

As the reader may wish to know something about the reading-room itself, a brief description of it may here be given. It is the room which in the picture appears to the right of the tower. It is forty feet in length and twenty-five feet in breadth, and is connected by a broad and beautiful arch with that part of the church which at present suffices for our sanctuary for public worship. A movable screen, placed beneath the arch, is all that separates the reading-room from the present audience room of the church, so that both rooms can easily be thrown into one whenever occasion requires. Lengthwise of the reading-room, in its central space, are placed two long tables, on one of which are found a variety of religious periodicals, and one clean secular newspaper. Some of the periodicals are printed in the vernacular languages, but the majority are English. Bibles and portions of the Scriptures in the vernaculars of this part of India and of other provinces also, as well as in English, Arabic, Persian and Sanskrit find a place upon this table. Ranged against the wall on one side of the room are four large book-cases containing the English books. Religious and other useful books in Urdu and Hindi—the vernaculars of this part of India—are not as numerous as we could wish, but still they comprise a goodly number, and we have the greater part of them in our library. Of all the books which our library contains, none is so much read as the Bible.

On the walls of the room are the two large Doré engravings—"Christ's Entry into Jerusalem," and "The Descent from the Prætorium"; also a large engraving, representing the "Condemnation of Huss"; together with fine portraits of Washington and Lincoln. Above

15

the portrait of "The Father of his Country" is fastened a small wooden hatchet, brought from Mount Vernon, and made possibly from a piece of a cherry-tree! On easels in two corners of the room are pictures of "Christ Before Pilate," and "The Ships of Columbus in Sight of Land." Chairs for visitors encircle the reading table, while an artistic clock of large size, and a fine American globe, mounted on a suitable stand, complete the furniture of this attractive room.

While writing the closing lines of this chapter, the appreciative remark of an English-speaking Hindu resident of Jhansi, who was invited to look at the reading-room when it was ready for use, and was told that the privileges which it afforded could be enjoyed by any one free of charge, is recalled. "This," said he, "is nothing but pure benevolence." We were glad to have from so intelligent a non-Christian man as he was, such a recognition of the true character of our missionary work in at least one of its departments.

The reading-room, which is well lighted, is kept open each week-day evening, this being the time when most persons can find leisure to visit it.

XXVI.

THE COMPLETION OF THE CHURCH, AND ITS DEDICATION, FEB. 27th, 1902.

As the church approached completion the agent of the contractors, to whom the workmen were immediately responsible, grew more and more negligent. My husband therefore determined to propose to the Allahabad firm that he would release them from any further responsibility for the building, and would himself undertake to finish it, in case such an arrangement should be entirely agreeable to them. They had uniformly acted in the most honorable manner in their dealings with us, and they now at once expressed their entire willingness to agree to my husband's proposal, saying at the same time that they were the more ready to be released from their obligation, since the work already done by them had been done at a loss, a fact about which they had up to that time kept silent.

It was just after the spire had been finished that my husband undertook to complete the building, and much work that required the most careful oversight then remained to be done both on the outside and in the inside of the structure. He would not at this time have voluntarily assumed such a burden, had not the taking up of this task, heavy as he knew it would be, seemed to him the lesser of two evils. We expected to leave India in a few months, and all the arrangements for our furlough to the United States had in the meantime to be made. It is hardly needful to say, that to do the thousand and one things which it was necessary for us to do before we left, in addition to getting the church ready for dedication, required all the exertion which it was possible for us to put forth.

As our church tower was completed, we desired to see it serving at the earliest possible date the special purpose for which it was erected. From the Mahomedan mosque the *muezzin* in sonorous accents calls the faithful to assemble for the purpose of reciting the prescribed *namaz*, which in English is misnamed prayer; and from the Hindu temple is heard the sound of the gong or conch, which is meant to inform not only the worshippers of the god, but the god himself, of what is going on at the sacred shrine. That from our church tower a sweet-toned bell should summon the worshippers of the true God to render unto him in his house the honor due to his name would be eminently proper, and we hoped to see such a bell hanging in the place made ready for it before the dedication of the building should take place.

We had no money with which to purchase it, but again the pen, of which at other times and for similar purposes use had been made, was set in motion, and our object was soon gained. A letter was sent to the Meneely Bell Company of Troy, N. Y., describing the kind of bell which we desired to procure, and telling them that if they could furnish it, we hoped they would allow us to pay for it in installments, as the money for this purpose was not in hand. They promptly replied that they were entirely willing to furnish the bell on the terms proposed, and at cost price, and it was soon sent. After hearing from Messrs. Meneely and Company, we wrote to that ever responsive Body, the Philadelphia Ladies' Board, to tell them that we had purchased a bell for our church tower that it was on its way to us from America, and that we had made ourselves personally responsible for the cost of it ; and we added that should any friend or friends feel interested in this investment and wish to share it with us, we should be most happy to allow them to do so. In response to this letter a generous contribution of about $ 70 was received, which very materially assisted us in meeting the responsibility we had incurred. As leisure was found for writing, various articles were sent to American papers, and the sums received in payment for these were applied to reduce the debt, until all that remained to be paid was the final installment, which was not a large amount, together with a part of the expense for transportation from Bombay to Jhansi.

Just at this time a letter came from a dear friend connected with the Fourth Presbyterian Church of Trenton, N. J., telling us of the death within a few weeks of each other of both her parents. They had been during their lives zealous and generous supporters both of home and foreign missions, and in the opening of Jhansi and the surrounding region to the Gospel had felt a deep interest. Our friend wrote that in remembrance of her parents, and as a thank-offering that they had been spared to her so long, she was sending us a sum of money to be expended in whatever way we might choose in connection with our work. We decided at once that a part of this sum should be used to complete the payment for the bell; and we had a use for the remainder which would be no less appropriate.

At the time when the walls of the church tower began to rise, it occurred to us that it would be well to leave spaces on its two outer sides, and at a suitable distance from its base, in which to insert white marble slabs bearing inscriptions of selected texts from the Word of God in the English, Hindi and Urdu languages in black letters so large and plain that they might be read without difficulty from the road passing the church. The truth which might never enter the ear, might thus catch the eye. Accordingly in the hope that we might sometime be able to get the desired tablets, places four feet in length, two feet in breadth, and two inches in depth, had been made ready for them.

When the remittance from our Trenton friend arrived, we found that after paying the balance due on the bell, there would be left in our hands from that gift a sufficient sum to meet the cost of one of the tablets. The means for obtaining the second tablet also were so soon provided that we were able to order both of them from Calcutta at the same time. The second tablet was to be in memory of one whom God took to himself in the morning of her days—Harriet B. Talmage, the younger of the two daughters of my only sister. She had been intensely interested in our work in India, and had sometimes in her letters expressed a desire to join us, but as her health had never been robust, we had not encouraged her to do this. After her departure a sum of money which was found in her purse, together with additions made by her father (her mother had preceded her to the heavenly home), her sister and a friend, was sent to us with the request that it be used in any way we desired as a memorial of the dear departed one. As I now look at the inscriptions upon this tablet, the loved one so early called away seems to be daily making known the Gospel, though her lips have long been closed.

As it may be interesting to the reader to know what the inscriptions upon these tablets are, they are here given. On one of them are the following texts, the first two being in English, the third in Persian-Urdu, and the fourth in Hindi:

Faithful is the saying, and worthy of all acceptation, that Christ Jesus came into the world to save sinners.

Believe on the Lord Jesus, and thou shalt be saved.

The wages of sin is death; but the free gift of God is eternal life in Christ Jesus our Lord.

In none other is there salvation: for neither is there any other name under heaven, that is given among men, wherein we must be saved.

On the other tablet are the following texts, likewise in English, Persian-Urdu and Hindi:

Come unto me, all ye that labor and are heavy laden and I will give you rest. Take my yoke upon you, and learn of me; for I am meek and lowly in heart: and ye shall find rest unto your souls.

Look unto me, and be ye saved, all the ends of the earth; for I am God, and there is none else.

God so loved the world, that he gave his only begotten Son, that whosoever believeth on him should not perish, but have eternal life.

Through the years it has been interesting to watch the people as they have been attracted by these tablets, and have paused to read the messages inscribed upon them. Those who daily pass by have become familiar with them, but strangers who can read are often seen standing before them singly or in groups, sometimes Hindus, sometimes Mahomedans, and occasionally a European. One day we saw an Englishman standing before the tablets. Seeing the doors of the reading-room open he entered. He was a stranger in India, he said. He told us how as he was walking through the city the sight of the beautiful church and the tablets had attracted his attention. He had been a wanderer through the earth, but did not tell us who he was. May it not be that the text in English, "Come unto me, all ye that labor and are heavy laden, and I will give you rest," was a message to his soul that day?

To aid us in praising God in his sanctuary when it should be ready for our use, an organ would be much needed. We had already deeply felt the necessity of obtaining an instrument for use in the English services which were being held in the school-house in the mission compound; and these services would, for the convenience of those who attended them, continue to be held there after the completion of the city church: so that our need in respect of an organ would soon be doubled. We had not thought of trying to procure at this time more than one instrument; but I shall now relate how, unexpectedly to us, two organs were provided for us.

Furnishing contributions as I was then doing for periodicals of the Presbyterian Board of Publication in Philadelphia, I received from time to time in acknowledgment of these contributions kind letters from Dr. Dulles, then secretary of this Board. Having been in former years a missionary in South India he had retained a warm interest in India missions, and seldom did a business letter come to me from him which did not contain some pleasant allusion to our circumstances, accompanied by the assurance that we and our work were frequently remembered by him. In the occupation of our new field he felt a deep interest. In the last letter sent to this valued friend, I alluded to our need of an organ for use in our religious services. This letter arriving after his death, fell into the hands of his successor, Dr. J. R. Miller, and when shortly after it was received, Dr. H. A. Nelson, at that time editor of "The Church at Home and Abroad," was calling at Dr. Miller's office, this gentleman taking up the letter addressed to Dr. Dulles, put it into the hands of Dr. Nelson, saying as he did so, "This letter, I am sure, will interest you."

Dr. Nelson, after reading the letter, laid it down with the remark, "I think I know where to get that organ for Mrs. Holcomb." This was not a merely momentary impulse. Action promptly followed, which resulted in the gift to us from the Southern Presbyterian Church of Independence, Missouri, of an excellent instrument, which in due time reached us in Jhansi, and is still doing good service in our church. Dr. Nelson had been for a time the highly esteemed pastor of the Church in Independence, and the people whom he had there served, and who held him in loving remembrance, were delighted to respond to his suggestion that they might do good by supplying that need of ours with which my letter had acquainted him, and them also through him.

When the news reached us of the death of our friend Dr. Dulles, not thinking that my letter to him, in which our need of an organ had been mentioned, might fall into the hands of others who would be interested in us, I wrote on the same subject to the ladies of the Philadelphia Board, and they with the promptitude which had marked all their actions in furtherance of our work, set about at once to enlist the interest of friends on our behalf, with the result that soon a very fine organ was sent to us. We had then a musical aid to devotion not only for our Hindustani, but for our English services as well, and thus the inconvenience of constantly moving a single instrument back and forth from one place to another was obviated. This second organ came from the Fourth Presbyterian Church of Trenton, N. J., which for more than thirty years has kindly permitted me to be their representative in the foreign field. From members of this Church have come at not infrequent intervals generous gifts for our work, with words of sympathy and cheer which have been like cordial in times of depressing anxiety.

While mentioning these organs donated to us, we take the opportunity of expressing our appreciation of a similar gift, a portable instrument, for use in camp and elsewhere, from the "West Hoboken Band," connected with the West Hoboken Presbyterian Church, New Jersey.

The need of a suitable communion service for our new church was not overlooked. This came as a most welcome gift from the Presbyterian Church of Girard, Pennsylvania, the home of my childhood. It is a beautiful silver-plated set of communion-ware, and bears upon it an inscription, which will serve to keep the donors in memory for long years to come.

While friends in America were thus aiding us, it must not be supposed that we had no friends nearer at hand. It is true that we have rarely had friends of our own denomination among our European neighbors in Jhansi, but we have found among them not a few members of the Church of England who have manifested a real interest in our work. One of these, the wife of Major Kelsall, of the Devonshire Regiment, then in Jhansi, deserves very special mention. This lady and I, on meeting, soon found that we had mutual friends, and our acquaintance, thus pleasantly begun, ripened into one of the warmest friendships of my Indian life. Just at the time when my acquaintance with her began, we greatly needed some one to preside at the organ and lead the singing at our Sabbath evening English service, and we determined to invite our newly-found friend to lend us her aid. This she very kindly consented to do, and following upon this took charge also of a week-day singing practice, giving herself to it with the greater alacrity, since the persons composing the choir were soldiers of her husband's regiment, in whose welfare she took a deep interest. She was an accomplished artist, and was accustomed to accompany her husband on his shooting excursions, when she would improve the opportunity to make studies of the wild flowers of the neighborhood. At length when the time came for her to leave India temporarily, she said to me, "I greatly desire to help you in the building of your church, but cannot at present make a contribution in money for this purpose. I will, however, while at home paint four panels of Jhansi wild flowers, and have them put together in a screen, which I will forward to any friend of yours in America, whom you may designate, to be sold for the benefit of your work." In due time the screen was made, and forwarded at our request to our friend, Dr. Henry M. Field of New York, who kindly undertook to dispose of it for us. The amount received for the screen, which must have been a marvel of beauty, was four hundred and ten dollars, after deducting the cost of transportation. The letter informing us of the sale of the screen, and containing a draft for the amount realised, reached Jhansi in time to enable us to send the news we had received to Mrs. Kelsall just as she was again setting foot upon the soil of India on her return from England. It cheered her greatly to hear that we had received for the product of her brush so goodly a sum.

Another lady residing in Jhansi, who gave us a liberal contribution for our church and reading-room, said when sending it, "I liked the way your husband put the matter before us, saying that he would be glad to receive a donation, if we desired to avail ourselves of the *privilege* of helping you in your enterprise."

While referring to such donations as these for our church, one or two contributions for our work may also be mentioned. At one time a Lieutenant of the garrison sent us five hundred rupees, $ 167, for the support of a zenana teacher. Another officer of the garrison requested me to send him our subscription book, remarking that he was accustomed to subscribe to the local mission wherever he was stationed, and regular subscriptions were received from him while he remained in Jhansi.

The members of our Hindustani congregation, who were able to help at all, were not backward in tendering their aid, but of their own accord brought to my husband their contributions to the church building fund.

Every seamstress knows how many stitches have to be taken in finishing a garment after it begins to look as if the making of it were completed. So it was in regard to the last things which required attention at the church, as we busied ourselves in completing the arrangements for the dedicatory service. It was an unspeakable comfort at such a time to have the kindly assistance which Mr. and Mrs. Griswold rendered us, and to know that the work from which we were about to withdraw for a season would be left in such capable hands. The audience-room of the church was at length furnished with seats, a temporary pulpit was provided, the organ was put in its place, the reading-room library, of which we were justly proud, was set in order in book-cases lent for the purpose until others could be provided, the reading table was supplied with periodicals and the Scriptures in various languages, the bell was hung in the tower, and the ground around the church was put in order.

The day and hour for the dedication having been set, invitations to be present on the occasion were sent to our friends in Jhansi, and to the members of our mission in other places. On account of the time and money it would cost them to come, because of the distances which separated us, none of our fellow missionaries were able to accept our invitation, except the Rev. J. S. Woodside. His coming was looked forward to with great pleasure on account of the very great interest he had felt in the opening up of the work at Jhansi. We were also to enjoy another great pleasure which we had not anticipated. Mrs. Scott, who had been for so many years the principal of the Woodstock school at Landour, in company with her daughter, was spending a part of her cold weather holiday within the bounds of the Furrukhabad Mission, with which in the earlier years of her missionary life she had been connected, and we received a note from her asking if it would be convenient for us to receive them for a brief visit. Nothing could have been more opportune than their proposal to visit us at this time, and accordingly they were urged to come at once, that they might enjoy with us the happy occasion then so near at hand. They accordingly came without delay. Never had we seen Mrs. Scott in apparently better health, or in more exuberant spirits. She had greatly enjoyed her visits to other stations of our mission, and manifested the liveliest interest in all she saw in Jhansi, and especially in our new church and reading-room. Observing that both my husband and myself were tired and worn, she said, "Leave to me and my daughter all care in regard to the decoration of the church for the dedicatory service. This will relieve you somewhat, and it will be a great pleasure to us to take charge of this part of the preparation." We gratefully accepted their kind offer, and enjoyed seeing them happy in doing what they could do so well. With potted palms and other plants, and with cut flowers supplied in abundance from our own garden and the gardens of friends, arranged by their artistic hands, both the church and reading-room were made most attractive. In all this decorative work Mrs. Scott was the guiding spirit. Her fine, strong face, which lighted up with enthusiasm as she moved about putting an artistic touch here and another there, looked almost youthful. While her mother was thus employed, her daughter, turning to me with a look of pride, said, "Isn't mamma splendid?"

We were greatly favored in having Miss Scott, the teacher of music in the Woodstock school, to preside at the organ at the dedicatory service. It was also gratifying to us that the Rev. J. F. Ullmann of our mission, to whom the Indian Church is indebted for a very large number of its best hymns, had manifested his interest in what we were doing by writing a hymn of dedication to be used at this time.

The wife of our magistrate had from the beginning been much interested in the progress of the work on our church, and when leaving for a visit to England had said, "I desire very much to be present when the church is formally dedicated, and therefore I cannot wish that it may be completed before my return to Jhansi." It was not finished until some time after her return. When a time had been appointed for the dedication—Saturday morning, February 27th, our friends the magistrate and his wife were invited to be present. They had made arrangements for a garden-party on their grounds in the afternoon of the same day and had invited us to be present with our guests. But late in the afternoon of Friday a telegram reached us from Mr. Woodside telling us that a change in the railway time-table, of which he had not known, had caused him to miss the night train from Agra to Jhansi, and requesting us, if we could, to postpone the dedication from Saturday morning until Saturday afternoon. We were much disappointed, but as Mr. Woodside was the only one of our own mission outside of Jhansi who could be present with us, and as he was on his way to us, we wished to accede to his request, if it should be found possible to do this. The arrangements of others besides ourselves had of course to be considered; but not without hope that a change in our plan might be made, my husband with the telegram in hand walked across the road to the magistrate's house. When he had made the wife of the magistrate acquainted with the situation of affairs, she at once said, "By all means postpone your service to the afternoon, if you can possibly do so; for to have the service proceed without Mr. Woodside, after all the trouble he has taken to be present, would be a great disappointment to him." "But what about *your* arrangements?" queried my husband. "I shall not miss being present," was the reply. "I shall at once send out notices to all who have been invited to our garden-party, informing them that it has been unavoidably postponed." And this she did, to her no small inconvenience, as all the arrangements for her entertainment had been made. We accordingly informed our English friends in regard to the postponement of the service, and communicated the same information to the members of our Hindustani congregation, who in turn made known the change to their non-Christian neighbors who desired to be present.

Saturday morning dawned brightly, as was to be expected at that time of the year. A restful forenoon was much enjoyed after the busy days which had preceded it, and early in the afternoon we had the pleasure of welcoming our friend for whose coming we had waited. The hour appointed for the dedication was 5 P.M., but going ourselves early to the church we found that people from the city, including our own people living there, had already begun to assemble. The members of our Christian congregation were naturally deeply interested in what was about to take place, while many non-Christians were present merely as on-lookers, attracted by curiosity. Among the non-Christians present on this occasion were some persons who were intelligent enough and also unprejudiced enough to feel some sort of sympathy with us as missionaries. Soon the reading-room and church-room, forming that day one audience-room, were filled with people. Very unique and interesting was this congregation, the first to gather together in the new sanctuary which God had given us. Among the Europeans present were representatives of the civil government, as well as military officers from the garrison. There were also with us visitors from abroad, one of them being Lord Radstock, who had been spending a few weeks in Jhansi engaged in quiet evangelistic work among his own countrymen; and another being an English lady of rank who was touring in India for the purpose of extending the work of the Young Women's Christian Association, then in its infancy in this country. The bell in the church tower had been ringing out its welcome to all, and when its sound ceased, the organ prelude hushed to silence the whole assembly, and the solemn but gladsome service began. Responsive readings of passages of the Scripture formed a part of the exercises. Hymns printed for the occasion had been distributed, enabling all who wished

CHURCH AND READING-ROOM COMPLETED.

to do so, to take part in praising God. The preliminary part of the service being ended, the object of the gathering was explained, and the dedicatory prayer was offered. Then followed the doxology—"Praise God from whom all blessings flow," and the benediction, after which the congregation dispersed.

Before leaving the church our European friends congratulated us on our having succeeded in building so attractive a sanctuary. Quite unexpectedly Lord Radstock had previously shown his interest in our enterprise by putting into my husband's hands a liberal contribution. As those who were particularly interested in the occasion still lingered in the church, Mrs. Scott stood at my side, her face all aglow with pleasure. She could not have been more interested, nor have felt a more genuine satisfaction, had the building been one connected with her own special work. When shortly after her return to Landour she was seized with an illness from which she did not recover, we felt that we had special cause to be thankful that so near the close of her earthly life we were privileged to have her with us to be a sharer of our joy.

At the conclusion of the dedicatory service the reading-room was inspected by the Indian gentlemen present, when one of them turning to my husband said, "God will bless you for this."

On the Lord's day morning following the dedication the Lord's Supper was administered in our new sanctuary, and in this a number of our European friends participated, including the visitors from England. On the afternoon of this day an evangelistic service was held in the church, when addresses were made both in English and Hindustani. One of those who spoke in Hindustani was Mr. Woodside, while Lord Radstock spoke in

English, the substance of his address being also given in Hindustani for the benefit of those who did not understand English.

Thus began and thus ended the first Sabbath services held in our house of prayer in the city of Jhansi, and there regular Christian worship on the Lord's day and on Wednesday afternoons has ever since been continued.

M. E. PRESS, MOUNT ROAD, MADRAS, 1905.

XXVII.

THE SELLING OF CHRISTIAN LITERATURE.

The preparation and dissemination of Christian literature is an indispensable auxiliary to the preaching of the Gospel in a heathen land. In this department of evangelistic effort the first place belongs to the translation, printing, and circulation of the Scriptures. It is essential, however, that this work be supplemented by the writing, publication, and dissemination of such tracts and books as shall serve to explain and illustrate the teachings of the Bible. For these purposes Bible Societies as auxiliaries of the British and Foreign Bible Society, and Tract Societies aided by the Religious Tract Society of London, were long ago established in a number of the chief business centres of India, as Madras, Calcutta, Bombay, Bangalore, Allahabad, and Lahore. Both in the translation of the Scriptures and in the writing of Christian tracts and books, the missionaries of the American Presbyterian Church have ever taken a prominent part, and either as honorary secretaries of the North India Bible and Tract Societies at Allahabad, or as members of the executive committees of these Societies and of those at Lahore, they have rendered important service to the cause of Christ.

It may not be generally known that at one time the Presbyterian Board of Foreign Missions had under serious consideration the plan of sending that great scholar, afterwards so eminent as a teacher in Princeton Theological Seminary, Joseph Addison Alexander, to India, to be stationed at Calcutta, the main object being the promotion of the cause of Christianity in India through the much-needed preparation of Christian literature suited to this country.

But however man's plans may fail, God's plans are carried into effect. The work of preparing Christian schoolbooks and general Christian literature for India, and of disseminating the same throughout the length and breadth of the land, was greatly promoted by a devoted man of God whose missionary life, extending through a period of sixty years, recently came to a close. This was John Murdoch, LL. D., whose writings and publications, even after he had passed the age of threescore and ten years, were multiplied to a prodigious extent. His biography soon to appear will reveal a life seldom if ever equaled for singleness of devotion to the cause of Christian missions. In passing, it may also be mentioned that to a like-minded brother of Dr. Murdoch, whose home was in far-away Australia, India owes a great debt, for at different times during John Murdoch's missionary career, there were sent to him by this brother to aid in the evangelization of India various sums of money, which in the aggregate amounted to no less than two hundred thousand dollars.

Interested as we had ever been in the circulation of Christian literature, the opportunity for efforts in this direction, which our new field afforded, very soon appeared to us to be exceptionably favorable. This was because there were so many persons, mostly men, in the city of Jhansi, who could read both Hindi and

Urdu, and also because so many of these understood the English language. We therefore speedily set about to improve our opportunity to the utmost. In the early days of missionary enterprise in India, the Scriptures and religious books, not to say tracts, were freely given away, as they could rarely be sold, but that condition of things long ago ceased to exist. Even the smallest tracts are now sold, though the price of a single tract may not exceed one-sixth of a cent, the only exception to the rule as regards the selling of tracts being the gratuitous distribution of leaflets. It is considered far better to sell at nominal prices a limited number of books and tracts than to distribute gratuitously a larger number, because the person who pays a price for a book will be more likely to prize it and preserve it carefully.

It was not enough that we should have in some central locality a book depôt where the Bible and other books in the different languages of Central India should be kept for sale. Our reading room in the city, open every day except Sunday, would answer for that purpose. A book hawker, who would go about among the people day by day and offer to them the books which we had for sale, was a necessity. A colporteur, therefore, was as soon as possible placed upon our staff of workers, and whenever through any cause his place fell vacant, we sought at once to fill it, for we greatly deprecated any interruption in this work.

The bookseller's field in Jhansi is not only the large native city, but it includes various centres of population outside the city wall within a radius of three miles; and the best opportunity of all has, through the courtesy of the railway officials, been found at the large railway station situated in the European quarter.

Crowds of people have been met in the railway carriages as the trains halted for a longer or shorter time, and also inside the station, the spacious waiting room for native passengers being usually full. Here on a cloth spread upon the floor the Bibles, New Testaments, and separate Gospels, together with a great variety of books and tracts in Hindi, Urdu, and English, suitable for all classes, could be exhibited and examined at leisure. The people of India buy Christian books more freely when away from home than at any other time, because they are then beyond the observation of their neighbors, and many a Bible, or Gospel, or other Christian book purchased by a traveler goes where the colporteur may never be sent.

Our sales of books and tracts has in the aggregate been very large. The Scriptures entire or in portions are frequently called for. And so day by day through our colportage agency the precious seed-corn of divine truth has been cast upon the waters in the assurance given us in God's Word that it shall be found again, it may be, after many days.

XXVIII.

OUR HOUSE AT RANIPUR.

The reader will remember the description in Chapter XII of our first tour in the Jhansi district. Eastward from Jhansi we reach the limit of our district at the fiftieth milestone on the left bank of the river Dhasan. The limit of our first tour was the town of Mau, forty miles from Jhansi. Ranipur is situated thirty-five miles east of Jhansi.

We have made tours from time to time in other directions, but the road between Jhansi and Mau has been traveled by us more frequently than any other road in our district, and we have been led to spend more time at Ranipur than at any other place on this road. This was because we found the large community of weavers in this town remarkably hospitable and tractable. For this reason, we at length decided to make Ranipur our headquarters at this end of our field, although Mau, only five miles distant from Ranipur, on account of its situation directly on the railway, its larger population, its fine buildings, its busy bazaars, and its general picturesqueness, was much more attractive. There was, moreover, at Mau, a very comfortable rest-house, provided for government officials, but available as well for the accommodation of other people. In fact, as regards Ranipur, there was nothing to attract us, except the greater promise of fruitfulness in our work.

When staying at Ranipur, in the cold season, we lived under canvas, pitching our tents under two very large shade trees at the forks of the road just outside the town, but we soon began to feel the need of a house, as without such a shelter it would be impossible for us to carry on our work there during the hot and rainy seasons, which comprise two-thirds of the year. To be able during eight long months to do nothing more for our out-station than to make flying visits to it from Mau, either early in the morning or toward the close of the day, seemed to be only an aggravation of our predicament.

As soon as possible, therefore, we began to collect money for the building of a house, and to look out for a suitable site on which to erect it. When at length we had in hand a thousand rupees, equal to three hundred and thirty-three dollars, for this purpose, it suddenly occurred to us that the old ruined fort on the river bank could be utilized by us to great advantage, if we could secure it for the mission. It belonged to the government, and possibly the authorities might be willing to sell it to us. Its massive walls would afford the most substantial foundations on which to build our house, while its outworks would furnish abundant materials in stone and bricks with which to rear our proposed dwelling. The more we considered it, the more pleased were we with our scheme in every respect.

In instituting negotiations for the purchase of this property, the magistrate of the district was the official with whom we had to deal, and fortunately for our cause, he, besides being our nearest neighbor in Jhansi, was exceedingly friendly to us, especially because he

BULLOCK CART FOR DISTRICT WORK.

and my husband had wrought together in relieving the sufferers in the district during the recent famine. In the cold season, following that time of suffering, it came about that my husband was the magistrate's guest for a day or two while both were touring in the district, and thus a good opportunity presented itself to broach the subject which for some time past had been of great interest to us.

On being made acquainted with our desire to buy the fort at Ranipur in case the government should feel disposed to sell it, the magistrate at once said that as the old fort was of no use to the government, he saw no reason why it should not be sold to us, and accordingly he set a day when he would meet my husband at Ranipur in order that after viewing the property, they might come to an understanding as to the next step to be taken towards its acquirement by us. At the appointed time the meeting took place, when the ruins were duly surveyed, and then the magistrate, after asking my husband how much he was prepared to give for the property, without waiting for an answer, said, in good-natured banter, "Will you give a thousand rupees for it?" In reply, my husband said: "I will tell you just how we are situated as to funds with which to provide ourselves with a house, and then you will be able to judge how much we can afford to give for this property. We have in hand, all told, about a thousand rupees for the site and the house." Hearing this he said: "Send your application for the purchase of the property to me, and in making an offer for it mention any sum you please." He then added, "I will suggest to the government that the fort be made over to you as a gift." No time was lost in placing in the magistrate's hands the written application, with the offer for the property of fifty rupees, or a little less than seventeen dollars, and in due course my husband was informed that his offer had bêen accepted, and that on receipt of the price named, the property would be secured to him.

As to the house as it now appears in the picture, in anticipation of being able soon to build it, my husband had purchased at auction in Jhansi, timbers of various kinds, besides doors, windows, and tiles, all of which materials, together with stone slabs for the roof, were transported to Ranipur at the beginning of the next cold season, when the work of building began. It was found to be much more difficult to carry on building operations in an out-of-the-way village than in Jhansi, for it was necessary to bring from Jhansi the skilled workmen who were needed, and to burn our own lime instead of buying it ready to our hand. When the weather grew too hot for my husband to live in his tent at Ranipur, he was obliged to take refuge in the rest-house at Mau, and to go from there each morning to direct the work. And when any exigency kept him at Ranipur until a late hour of the forenoon, as was very often the case, then it was necessary for him to face the hot wind as well as to bear the burning heat of the sun during an hour's drive before he could reach his breakfast. By mid-summer the house was completed, but not without the expenditure of more money than we had in hand for the building when we began, in which additional expense, however, the mission was in no way involved.

The house consists of two main rooms built upon the terrace of the old fort, together with a room in the upper portion of the middle tower, and a bath-room—an indispensable provision in an Indian dwelling.

OUR HOUSE AT RANIPUR.

Then on the same level with the house a broad covered veranda extends along the whole inner front, its floor forming the flat roof which covers two rooms whose walls were built up from the ground. This veranda serves the purpose of a chapel for the public worship of God. One of the outer towers has been converted into a store-room, and the other is used as a cook-house. Steps lead up from the ground to the terrace on both sides of the house. The new rooms below are occupied by the native minister and his wife, while other quarters on the ground level have been fitted up for his helpers.

Thus has the old Bundela fort been entirely revolutionized, and from it as a centre Gospel light will, we trust, long continue to radiate. It was built about three hundred years ago by Princess Hiradeva, a famous Rani of Orcha, who founded the town of Ranipur.